Muslims

Their Religious Beliefs and Practices

Volume 1 The Formative Period

The Library of Religious Beliefs and Practices
Edited by: John Hinnells, University of Manchester, and Ninian Smart,
University of California Santa Barbara

Already published:

The Ancient Egyptians: Their Religious Beliefs and Practices
A. Rosalie David

Jews: Their Religious Beliefs and Practices
Alan Unterman

The Sikhs: Their Religious Beliefs and Practices
W. Owen Cole and Piara Singh Sambhi

Zoroastrians: Their Religious Beliefs and Practices
Mary Boyce

*Theravāda Buddhism: A Social History from
   Ancient Benares to Modern Colombo*
Richard Gombrich

The British: Their Religious Beliefs and Practices
Terence Thomas

Mahāyāna Buddhism
Paul Williams

This series provides pioneering and scholarly introductions to different
religions in a readable form. It is concerned with the beliefs and practices
of religions in their social, cultural and historical setting. Authors come
from a variety of backgrounds and approach the study of religious beliefs
and practices from their different points of view. Some focus mainly on
questions of history, teachings, customs and ritual practices. Others
consider, within the context of a specific region or geographical region,
the inter-relationships between religions; the interaction of religion and
the arts; religion and social organization; the involvement of religion in
political affairs; and, for ancient cultures, the interpretation of
archaeological evidence. In this way the series brings out the multi-
disciplinary nature of the study of religion. It is intended for students of
religion, ideas, social sciences and history, and for the interested
layperson.

Muslims

*Their Religious Beliefs
and Practices*

Volume 1 The Formative Period

Andrew Rippin

ROUTLEDGE

London and New York

First published 1990
by Routledge
11 New Fetter Lane, London EC4P 4EE

Simultaneously published in the USA and Canada
by Routledge
a division of Routledge, Chapman and Hall, Inc.
29 West 35th Street, New York, NY 10001

© 1990 Andrew Rippin

Set in Garamond 3 by Columns of Reading
Printed in Great Britain by
Richard Clay Ltd, Bungay, Suffolk

British Library Cataloguing in Publication Data
Rippin, Andrew
  Muslims.
  Vol. 1 : The formative period
  1. Islam
  I. Title   II. Series
  297
  ISBN 0–415–04518–5
  ISBN 0–415–04519–3 pbk

Library of Congress Cataloging in Publication Data
Rippin, Andrew, 1950–
  Muslims : their religious beliefs and practices / Andrew Rippin.
    p.   cm. — (The Library of religious beliefs and practices)
  Bibliography: p.
  Includes index.
  Contents: v. 1. The formative period.
  ISBN 0–415–04518–5. — ISBN 0–415–04519–3 (pbk.)
  1. Islam.   I. Title   II. Series.
BP161.2.R53   1990
297—dc20   89–10442

To Marion
partner in the Two-way Waltz

Contents

Preface

In teaching undergraduate students, I have often encountered individuals who come to the study of Islam with a background in the historical study of the Hebrew Bible or early Christianity, and who express surprise at the lack of critical thought that appears in introductory textbooks on Islam. The notion that 'Islam was born in the clear light of history' still seems to be assumed by a great many writers of such texts. While the need to reconcile varying historical traditions is generally recognized, usually this seems to pose no greater problem to the authors than having to determine 'what makes sense' in a given situation. To students acquainted with approaches such as source criticism, oral formulaic composition, literary analysis and structuralism, all quite commonly employed in the study of Judaism and Christianity, such naive historical study seems to suggest that Islam is being approached with less than academic candour.

In recent years, however, scholarly analyses of Islam have started to broaden their methodological perspectives. There has especially been a trend away from historical positivism (a notion already disposed of in a great many fields) and a move toward an approach which attempts to take into account the literary character of the so-called historical sources. This new effort has resulted in a recognition of the ideological aspects of the literary texts involved; central has been the critical appreciation of the attempts made in the texts to define and legitimize an understanding of Islam where the religion functions as a normative system which acts, in a convenient and stabilizing manner, to legitimate the right to rule of a certain group of people. Islam is, of course, a 'religion' in the common meaning of the word; the character that the system has adopted in its tenets and practices, however, can be seen in many instances to reflect an ideological significance for its society.

The picture of Islam which results from this mode of research leaves a great deal of ambiguity concerning precisely what can be known of the very early times. What must be recognized is the nature of the source material in which one sees a theological/ideological backreading of history. As a result, what one can know, and what will be explored and emphasized in this book, is how Muslims from the early ninth century onwards (when the documentation of Islam becomes fully available) viewed the history of their own religion and how they developed that understanding into the various manifestations of 'orthodox' Islam. Given the scope and length of this book, in most instances it has only been possible to sketch out the issues rather than actually argue the proof for them as fully as may be desirable. Some Islamicists may well feel that this book has glossed over too many details which are crucial in the debate over sources and its implications. Yet it seems to me that the attempt to write a very general textbook such as this, one which paints its picture in very large brush strokes and suggests, in some places at least, a modified view of the accepted version of the emergence of Islam, is worthwhile and potentially fruitful for students. Certainly there seems to be no good reason to withhold the basic approach from this audience, especially since the methodological assumptions underlying it are so commonplace in the study of other religions. As well, it must also be kept in mind that in no sense does this book attempt to provide an entire 'history of Islam'. Rather, the attempt has been made to outline the emergence of the mature formulation of the various facets of the religion. Within that maturation process, some elements took longer than others to reach a relatively stable form and therefore no definitive cut-off point can be stipulated for marking the end of the 'formative' period covered by this work. Likewise, this book does not attempt to take into its purview the expansion of Islam into the many different regions of the world. The intellectual struggles which played a vital part in the emergence of Islam as the religion we have come to know, appear to have taken place in the Islamic 'heartland' of the Arabo-Persian empire; it is to that region, then, that the major attention must be paid.

The title of this book, *Muslims, their religious beliefs and practices*, should not be taken to imply that a static entity, subject to description, composed of 'Muslims', actually exists or has ever existed. Rather, there exists a religious group of people, and like all peoples, it has moved through and been influenced by (as well as being an influence on) history, although recapturing that history in words may well be almost impossible. So the 'religious beliefs and practices of Muslims' is not a single entity but rather something which has changed over time, has moved with the historical circumstances and has varied for reasons which sometimes are very obscure. As a religion, Islam is also a phenomenon in which people believe and which has created its own sense of historical development. But this Muslim sense of the past has varied over time according to the needs of the situation. To try, therefore, to understand this picture is, once again, the task of this book. Furthermore, central to the presentation of the 'religious beliefs and practices of Muslims' is the idea of 'identity': that is, how a religion functions on both a personal and social level to provide that 'stable niche in a predictable environment'.[1] The role Islam has played, and continues to play, in creating and developing an understanding of the world and of the relationship between individuals is vital; yet this too is not an unchanging mechanism but one which has gradually and subtlely changed in response to the realities and pressures of the world. To try to understand this role of the sense of Islamic identity and the ways in which this role has responded to the needs of the situation is also the task of this study.

The material which must be dealt with is fairly complex, but the basic notions underlying it all are straightforward enough. Islam, as the religion of the people known as Muslims, is held to have been revealed by God, the same God who revealed Himself to the Jews and the Christians, the one true God known in Arabic as Allah, to a native of the Hijaz on the Western side of the Arabian peninsula by the name of Muhammad ibn 'Abd Allah, in the beginning of the seventh century CE. Over a period of twenty-two years, a scripture which was called the Qur'an (=Koran) was revealed to Muhammad by God. A work roughly the same length as the New Testament, the book calls on polytheists along with the Jews and the Christians to declare and put into action their commitment to God's final revealed religion. Heaven awaits those who heed the call, a fiery damnation in hell for those who ignore it. Clearly it is a message which fits within the overall Judeo-Christian tradition and, at the same time, is one which sees the whole world as eventually having to respond one way or the other to its call.

Illustrations

Acknowledgements

The translations from the Qur'an used in this book are taken from T. B. Irving (al-Hajj Ta'lim 'Ali), *The Qur'an. The First American Version* (Brattleboro, VT, Amana Books, 1985) and are used by permission of the publisher. As is the way in scholarship, Dr Irving may well disagree with some of the interpretations of Islam presented in this book. However, I do trust that he will understand that my use of his translation is intended as a complement to his attempt to express the meaning of the Qur'an in a way which will prove meaningful within the context of the modern world. In citing the Qur'an, the verse numbering of the Arabic text known as the Cairo edition (as used by Dr Irving) is employed. Readers using other translations of the text, such as that of A. J. Arberry, will find a slight variation in the numbering scheme. In citing the Qur'an, the form: 'chapter (*sura*) number' / 'verse number' is employed.

Conversation and correspondence with a number of friends have helped me tremendously in the writing of this book. N. Calder, G. R. Hawting, B. T. Lawson, F. MacKay and A. A. M. Shereef have all attempted to guide me in crucial ways, helping to moderate the expression of my ideas when necessary, frequently stimulating me to further thought. I offer my sincere thanks to them. John Hinnells has been of great assistance in his position as editor of this series, constantly reminding me of the intended audience of the book and of my responsibilities to those readers. The extent to which it may be judged that I have succeeded in making this book accessible to students and other non-initiates is, in no small measure, due to his urgings, for which I am most grateful.

Transliteration and other technical considerations

Considerations of printing costs have not allowed diacritical marks to be included in the Arabic words and names cited in this book. For further information on any given topic, or a more precise rendering of a given Arabic word, the reader should refer to the *Encyclopaedia of Islam* (Leiden: E.J. Brill, first edition 1913–36; reprinted 1987 as new edition, 1960– up to the letter 'm' so far; *Shorter Encyclopaedia of Islam*, 1953, gathers together articles on religion from the old edition with some updated material). This essential reference tool is arranged according to the Arabic terms and this often seems a hindrance for readers not well acquainted with the subject; therefore, an attempt has been made in this book to include the relevant Arabic words in order to facilitate further reference through the *Encyclopaedia of Islam*. A problem arises, however, which makes this task somewhat more difficult than it should be. The transliteration system used in the *Encyclopaedia of Islam* is, in several instances, not that most commonly used in English-language books; simply to use the *Encyclopaedia of Islam* system here would perhaps encourage further confusion when readers consult other texts or when they try to correlate what is in this book to what they already know. This book, therefore, follows the system employed in the new edition of the *Encyclopaedia of Islam*[2] except for the letter 'j' (*jim*) and 'q' (*qaf*). For 'j' the Encyclopaedia uses 'dj', so, for example, an entry for *hajj* ('pilgrimage') will be found under *hadjdj*, or *jihad*, 'holy war', under *djihad*. For 'q', the Encyclopaedia uses 'k' with a subscript dot, thus intertwining the entries with 'k' representing the letter *'kaf'*. The reader must remember that where 'q' is found in a word in this book, the Encyclopaedia entry will have a 'k'. Examples are *qadi/kadi* ('judge') *tariqa/tarika* ('Sufi brotherhood') or *Qur'an/Kur'an*.

All dates are cited according to the 'Common Era' (CE), numerically equivalent to Christian AD.

Historical time chart

622	MUHAMMAD's move to Medina – the *hijra*
632	death of MUHAMMAD
634	death of ABU BAKR, first caliph
644	death of 'UMAR, second caliph
656	death of 'UTHMAN, third caliph
661	death of 'ALI, fourth caliph and figurehead of the Shi'ites
661	MU'AWIYA becomes caliph
661–750	UMAYYAD dynasty
680	death of caliph MU'AWIYA
	death of HUSAYN, son of 'Ali
685–705	rule of caliph 'ABD AL-MALIK
750	'ABBASID dynasty begins
765	death of Shi'ite Imam JA'FAR AL-SADIQ
767	death of jurist ABU HANIFA
	death of historian IBN ISHAQ
795	death of jurist MALIK IBN ANAS
813–33	rule of caliph AL-MA'MUN
820	death of jurist AL-SHAFI'I
855	death of jurist AHMAD IBN HANBAL
870	death of *hadith* collector AL-BUKHARI
875	death of *hadith* collector MUSLIM IBN AL-HAJJAJ
874	12th Imam MUHAMMAD AL-MAHDI in 'lesser occultation'
910	death of mystic AL-JUNAYD

922	death of mystic AL-HALLAJ
935	death of theologian AL-ASH'ARI
941	12th Imam MUHAMMAD AL-MAHDI in 'greater occultation'
944	death of theologian AL-MATURIDI
945	BUWAYHIDS take over Baghdad
1111	death of mystic AL-GHAZZALI

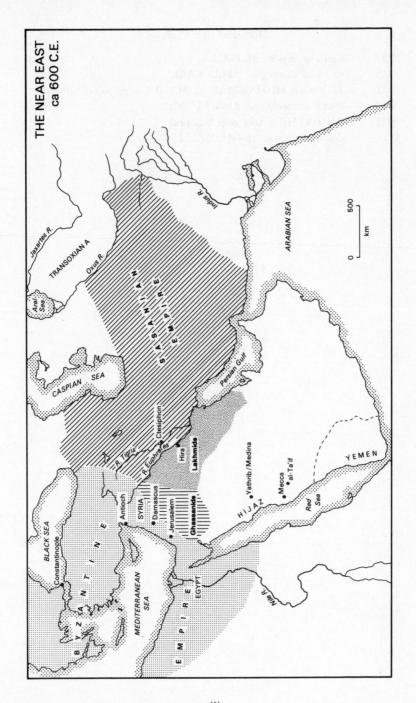

THE NEAR EAST
ca 600 C.E.

TRANSOXIANA

Jaxartes R.

Oxus R.

Aral Sea

Indus R.

ARABIAN SEA

500

0

km

CASPIAN SEA

S A S A N I A N   E M P I R E

R. Tigris

Ctesiphon

R. Euphrates

Hira

Lakhmids

Persian Gulf

YEMEN

BLACK SEA

Constantinople

Antioch

SYRIA

Damascus

Jerusalem

Ghassanids

HIJAZ

Yathrib/Medina

Mecca

al-Ta'if

Red Sea

B Y Z A N T I N E   E M P I R E

MEDITERRANEAN SEA

EGYPT

Nile R.

PART ONE

Structural elements for the formation of Islam

CHAPTER ONE

Pre-history

The foundations of Islam

Common wisdom would suggest that in order to understand the foundation of Islam we must have some knowledge of the historical, social, political and economic context from which the religion emerged. As a generalization, of course, this has a degree of validity. However, it is quite possible to question the value of this type of historical contextualization because it is highly dependent upon a notion of the religion of Islam existing as a conceptually defined entity from the very beginning of its proclamation. A more stimulating model of the foundation of Islam pictures the religion as emerging gradually, coming to a fixed sense of identity (and all that entails in terms of sources of authority) over a period of some two centuries. Certainly the gradual intertwining of developing Islamic ideology and its immediate environment presents a complex and confused picture, and thus a sketch of the political and religious situation in the Near East in the sixth through the eighth centuries will definitely help to put some of the matter in focus. The provision of such information should not be taken, however, in the sense of looking for 'influences upon Muhammad' from this pre-Islamic period (as so many studies of Islam seem to suggest) but rather as an attempt to sketch the context in which Islam did eventually emerge and to see the combination of factors in the society that made the religion successful and made it into the religion that it is today. While the point

3

may seem surprising at first, the relevance of the geographical region of Central Arabia to that emergent definition of what we have come to know as the religion of Islam is highly questionable; Islam (in its clearly defined and developed form) had its formative developing period outside the Arabian context and while the initial impetus for the religion is clearly tied to the Hijaz in Arabia, the character the religion adopted was moulded by more widespread Near Eastern precedents than would appear historically possible within the narrow isolation of Arabia.

The Near East before Islam

There are three foci of interest in the centuries preceding the wave of Arab conquests of the Near East region in the seventh century. The Christian Byzantines had some influence over the Red Sea, extending at times to an alliance with the Monophysite Christians of Abyssinia; the Zoroastrian Persians, with their capital in Ctesiphon in Mesopotamia, had influence which reached at times the eastern side of Arabia and along the south coast to the Yemen; and the South Arabian kingdoms whose fluctuating fortunes, last manifested in the Himyar dynasty of the sixth century, had lost virtually all semblance of vitality by the time of the rise of the Arabs. The Arabian peninsula, although having had settled centres for several millennia, did not contain a power to be reckoned with in the world at the time, except in so far as various tribal areas became pawns in the hands of external kingdoms, perhaps thereby creating the forces which would eventually expand out of the peninsula and subjugate the earlier rulers.

In the year 527 Justinian came to the throne of the Byzantine empire at Constantinople. He was determined to restore the unity with the decaying Roman empire, the western parts of which had been lost to the Germanic tribes, especially the Vandals and the Goths. He was successful in directing the reconquest of Italy, North Africa and part of Spain but, by his death in 565, much of this accomplishment was being nullified as the result of continual local uprisings. The Persians took advantage of the subsequent unstable situation and made initiatives on their western border with Byzantium. Heavy taxes, however, provoked instability on the edges of this newly expanded area. Heraclius, the Byzantine leader who died in 641, managed to gain supremacy in Constantinople in 610, only to witness the Persians taking Antioch in 613, Jerusalem in 614 and then marching into Egypt in 619. An attempt to move on Constantinople itself in the year 626 left the Persians disorganized and over-stretched.

Before this final move by the Persians, Heraclius had begun a counterattack and had successfully invaded Persian territory as far as Ctesiphon in 628, capturing Jerusalem in 629, forcing a retreat on the part of the Persian empire and causing eventually the murder of Shah Khusro II. The over-confident Byzantines relaxed and fell victim to the Arab conquest, which started most significantly with the initial capture of Damascus in 635.[1]

The situation in the Arabian peninsula

From the point of view of Arabia, this political situation was further confused and made more unstable by two additional factors: the interaction of the Arabs with the two major world powers and the religious rivalry between Jews, the various sects of Christians and, to a lesser extent, Zoroastrians.

Through a system of states functioning as tributaries to the Byzantines and Persians, the nomads of Arabia were kept within the confines of the desert area, and thus did not pose any great danger to the frontier area. As well, these tributary states, Hira (whose people are also known as the Lakhmids) under the Persians in the north-east of Arabia, and Ghassan under the Byzantines in the north-west, provided troops to their respective overlords. By the sixth century, these areas were composed of settled bedouin tribes and Christianity especially was making its presence felt;[2] these Arabs were, however, of little practical consequence to the world powers of the time, although towards the end of the sixth century, independence was seized by the Ghassanids, while the Lakhmids were forced into an even more subservient relationship with the Persians than had previously been the case. Overall, the tributary system, while it had been in operation for a number of centuries by the time of the Arab conquests, was becoming increasingly unstable in this period.

In the south of Arabia, inter-tribal warfare was bringing an end to the Himyar kingdom, the last in a long line of impressive states in the area of the Yemen. One of the reasons for the gradual decline in this region was the diminishing importance of the incense trade in the fourth century, in the wake of the Christian take-over of the pagan world and the weakening of the Roman economy.[3] South Arabia, the major source of incense for the world from antiquity (at least since the seventh century BCE), had based a great deal of its economy on the production and trade in this material which was used in Greco-Roman religious festivals and in medicinal preparations. With the shift in the world situation, this economy suffered greatly. Some scholars have also suggested that around the year 300 CE the whole area of Arabia suffered a drought, bringing about a collapse of the traditional agricultural basis of the local economy, although the evidence for this is not overwhelming.

Religion in the Arabian peninsula

The sedentary lifestyle of South Arabia had produced a society deeply involved in the various religious systems of the ancient Near East. Evidence, coming from inscriptions, reflects a developed stage of this religious growth and we have no information on how this religious system actually came about. Clearly, the area was closely linked to the Mediterranean and Mesopotamian worlds. Until the fourth century, all of the evidence points to the existence of a polytheistic religion with a northern Semitic character. The worship of 'Athtar, a male god who was the most prominent of the pantheon, is often said to have been related to the Ishtar cult of the north, whose female god was said to manifest herself in the Venus star. There were a number of other prominent deities whose identity varied with the locality and the historical era. Keeping these different deities clear and distinct is extremely difficult, given the complexities of dealing with the inscriptional source material, but a few observations can be made. The moon god was variously known as Ilmaqah, 'Amm, Sin and Wadd (the name of the latter is also known from Qur'an 71/23) and the sun goddess was known as Shams.[4] These gods and several others were held to be tribal patrons. As well, deities of the clan and the family also existed and these were often described simply as 'the god [*'lh*] of so-and-so'. Each level of deity was seen to govern over a different sphere, each in a power relationship to the next level: personal to village to tribal land to world. According to the evidence of archaeological remains from various temples, sacrifices were a prominent part of religious worship: incense offerings on stone altars and blood offerings were likely to have played a role. All these activities took place within temples which were apparently attended by both men and women, with the purpose of the rituals being seen as the acquisition of the benefits which these various gods could bestow. Other features attested by inscriptions include pilgrimage activities, ritual meals and a code of personal purity.

In the fourth or fifth century, South Arabian inscriptions start to speak of a monotheistic cult of Rahmanan, 'the Merciful', frequently qualified as 'Lord of heaven and earth'.[5] Very little evidence is found in the inscriptions for a continuation of the earlier polytheistic cult (although since inscriptions necessarily reflect an élite and official segment of society, whether the general populace so quickly gave up its polytheistic belief is open to question). Apparently the rise of the Himyarite kingdom in about the year 380 marks this change, coming about probably as a result of, or in order to accomplish, a unification of the various South Arabian tribes. The monotheistic impetus is often seen to be a result of Jewish influence in the society, although some scholars wish to see this as a natural, independent development (based on an evolutionary picture of religion in general). Some scholars also wish to connect this development to the Qur'anic notion of a *hanif*, the quality of being a monotheist in the face of paganism; to sustain such an interpretation, however, one must see in that Qur'anic term a designation of a historical reality rather than a spiritual one, a somewhat doubtful supposition. The Biblical echoes found in some of the monotheistic inscriptions, such as the phrase 'the Merciful [*rahmanan*], who is in heaven' and the use of a grammatical plural in reference to God (as in the Hebrew *elohim*) found in the inscriptional statement 'the God(s) to whom belong the heaven and earth' suggest that Judaism is the most likely influence on the formation of this cult. Little is known of the religious character of this monotheistic trend, so additional information is not available to settle the matter definitively. It is likely that Judaism was supported by the Persians as a tool against Byzantine influence in the south of Arabia.

Certainly, Judaism was present within this period of the monotheistic cult and perhaps even predated it slightly. There is clear and explicit evidence of a Jewish presence in South Arabia, attested towards the end of the fourth century. References are found to the 'community of Israel' as well as 'Lord of Jewry'. The presence of Jews in the Yemen continued until the mid-twentieth century when most were removed to the newly-formed State of Israel.

Christianity, meanwhile, was not in evidence in South Arabia before the sixth century, at which time it appears to have been present in a community centred in the town of Najran; it is thought to have spread there from Abyssinia. Accounts are found of persecution of the Christians early in the sixth century by the Jewish ruler Yusuf As'ar, probably as a result of fears of Byzantine influence over the Christian community. Sixth century retaliations by Abyssinian troops seem to mark the demise of Judaism as a power, with inscriptions thereafter speaking of belief in 'God and His Messiah and the Holy Spirit' on the part of the rulers. There is no doubt that the Christianity which spread from Abyssinia was supported by the Byzantines against Persian influence in the area, even though it was, from the Byzantine perspective, of the heretical Monophysite persuasion. By the end of the sixth century, the Persians started to encourage Nestorian Christianity, another strain of that faith which was abhorrent to both the Byzantines and the Abyssinians, and aided the Yemenites in their removal of the Abyssinian overlords. The country was so fractured and destroyed by being subject to the manipulation of the various foreign powers that little remained by the time of the rise of the Arabs to be of any particular significance to either major world power.

The significance of Central Arabia

The area of central Arabia remains a vast unknown territory during this historical period, of little significance to anyone in the ancient world except as a natural barrier of desert. Despite the extensive work done by scholars studying early Muslim literary texts concerned with the subject (archeological digs have not been permitted in crucial religious areas), the evidence for the role of the region as a focal point for a rich and economically explosive trade between south Arabia and the fertile crescent, as was once suggested, is virtually non-existent.[6] Any solid evidence of the religious character of the region reveals a polytheistic system having basic features in common with Semitic religion in general; this includes worship of gods associated with the astral cults and beliefs in spirits inhabiting rocks, trees and the like.[7] The role of Mecca as a sanctuary is fairly evident, although the character of this sacred area becomes rather muddled as a result of the manipulations of the data by later historians who have overlaid what would appear to be native Arabian sanctuary traditions with Jewish ones.[8]

Overall, given this situation, a number of things become clear in historical retrospect. Politically, the area of the Near East was unsettled at the time of the Arab conquests and was certainly in a condition which would allow for the emergence of a new configuration in political power. The interaction which did occur between the Arabs and the world at large saw the tribes being manipulated by the foreign policy of the empires, with no particular significance being given to the people themselves; this was true both in the north and in the south. The connection between the ancient empires and their religions was close, meaning that a new religious dispensation, separate from the notions connected with the old regimes, may well have found itself in a favorable position.

8

Pre-history in Muslim identity

There is far more significance to the pre-Islamic period than the preceding interpretation of historical data would seem to suggest, however. In terms of Muslim identity, the pre-Islamic period serves most emphatically as a historical, ideological and ethical counterpoint to the Islamic ethos. It is, therefore, an era in which Muslim writers have tended to be very interested and they have provided an abundant amount of material purporting to portray the period. From the standpoint of attempting to comprehend the foundation of the Islamic religion, then, the Muslim understanding of the period takes on a crucial and considerable role. The appreciation of this Muslim view, however, must be distinguished from reconstructing the history of the era itself; what is at issue here is the role of understanding the past and the kinds of pressures and interpretations to which such understanding becomes subject. This process, embodied within the Muslim understanding of the past, is one which is common to humanity: the recreation of the past embodied in the idea of 'tradition', selectively formed and reshaped into a new and relevant context.[9]

The notion of 'jahiliyya'

The pre-Islamic period is an era contrasted to the time and ethos of Islam, a contrast which is embodied in the term *jahiliyya*. This term is found in the Qur'an four times in reference to the idea itself and ten times in reference to people, as well as being used in verbal derivations related to the word with the same sense; the word would appear to be used in the book as the opposite of 'Islam', in that those who are connected to the *jahiliyya* are 'ignorant of God' – at least this is the way most Muslim commentators on the Qur'an have taken the word. For example, Qur'an 48/26 states: *While those who disbelieved were setting up fanaticism, the fanaticism of Ignorance {jahiliyya} in their own hearts, God sent His serenity down upon His messenger and on believers, and obliged them to respect the formula of heedfulness.* The religious accomplishment of Islam, the 'serenity' of this passage, can only be judged by comparing it to what came before it. Even more significantly, the impulse to demonstrate this accomplishment of Islam appears to rest ultimately upon the desire to prove the divine status of the religious dispensation itself: what Islam has accomplished in transforming society from *jahiliyya* to 'serenity' is in fact proof of the divine nature of the religion.

A consequence of this apparent impulse to illustrate the separation between *jahiliyya* and Islam is that a large amount of material emerged which was designed to prove and provide the appropriate pre-Islamic contrast. The starting point of all this material was, of course, the Islamic position – that is, only what was needed in order to provide this counterpoint to Islamic values is presented in the texts. In no sense do the Islamic sources attempt to provide a dispassionate presentation of pre-Islamic society, politics and religion (although many recent scholars of Islam have certainly attempted to take the material and recreate that era, despite the selectivity and biases of the material itself).

Discontinuity of Islam with the past

How this approach to portraying the past works can most easily be illustrated through an example dealing with a point of law. In legal issues, the impulse to demonstrate the benefits of Islam are quite pronounced for this often reflects very tangible elements within everyday Muslim life. Qur'an 2/168 reads: *Mankind, eat anything lawful, wholesome that exists on earth, and do not follow in Satan's footsteps; he is an open enemy of yours.* Common to a number of sources which deal with interpretation of the Qur'an and which provide anecdotes about the 'context' of the revelation of a verse[10] is the following: 'This verse was revealed about Thaqif, Khuza'a and 'Amir ibn Sa'sa'a who prohibited to themselves cultivated produce and grazing livestock. They also forbade the *bahira*, *sa'iba*, *wasila* and *hami* camels.'[11] The picture that is painted is one of various people before the revelation of the Qur'an doing things, in this case prohibiting to themselves various foods, which were to be permitted under the Islamic dispensation. Of course, it is not possible to prove that this was not actually so, that this event did not 'really happen', but that is not the point; what is of interest is how the anecdote works within the Islamic context, for the function of such stories would seem to be the prime reason Muslim writers transmitted such accounts: the purpose of the anecdote is to provide a measure of the accomplishment of Islam and to differentiate Islam clearly from what existed previously.

In fact, it is quite possible to demonstrate in individual cases that later Muslims did not know the 'facts' of the pre-Islamic period but rather that the anecdotes emerged for the purpose of anchoring Islam to history more firmly; other writers have provided many lucid examples of this phenomenon[12] and further instances are easy to locate. Concerning Qur'an 2/158, *Safa and Marwa are some of God's waymarks. Anyone who goes on*

Pilgrimage to the House or visits {it} will not be blamed if he runs along between them, anecdotes are repeated which speak of the pre-Islamic practices concerning the hills of Safa and Marwa but they are unclear as to whether the pre-Islamic Arabs did or did not run between them. One anecdote reads as follows:

> On Safa was the image of a man called Isaf, while on Marwa was the image of a woman called Na'ila. The People of the Book [i.e. the Jews and Christians] claimed that these two had committed adultery in the Ka'ba [in Mecca] so God converted them into stone and placed them on Safa and Marwa in order to act as a warning to others. . . . The people of the *jahiliyya* stroked the idols when they circumambulated them [during their pilgrimage rituals]. When Islam came and the idols were broken, Muslims detested the circumambulation between the hills because of [their association with] the idols. So God revealed this verse.[13]

Another explanation of the verse is found in this report:

> 'Urwa ibn al-Zubayr said to 'A'isha: 'I see no fault in someone who does not run between Safa and Marwa, nor would it concern me if I did not run between them'. 'A'isha answered: 'You are wrong, O son of my sister! Muhammad ran between them and so did the Muslims. Rather it was [the pagans] who sacrificed to Manat, the idol of Mushlal, who did not run between them. Then God sent down this verse. If it were as you say, the verse would read "there is no blame on whoever does not run between them".'[14]

Illustrated in these anecdotes is the ambivalence of the information. Either the pre-Islamic Arabs did or did not run between the two hills. Both reports certainly provide a justification for the Muslims running between them (which, after all, is the central question for later Muslim jurists) and at the same time, both reports provide a contrast with the pre-Islamic period. This contrast, note, can be positive or negative – either things are different from the past or they are the same. A similar phenomenon can be seen in many legal discussions, for example regarding foods being prohibited to Muslims 'by virtue of not being eaten by pre-Islamic Arabs'[15] where the evaluation as compared to the past is positive once again.

The role of the Abrahamic myth

In general, it can be said that this pre-Islamic material was not recorded with 'historical' reasons in mind, if by that we mean modern principles of historical research. Rather, the accounts were transmitted and written down in order to provide the necessary information for understanding the Qur'an specifically and for evaluating Islam as a whole. A very popular work is that written by Hisham ibn al-Kalbi who died in 819, and entitled *The Book of Idols*. The text gathers together poetical references to various 'pre-Islamic' deities, especially those cited in the Qur'an. Once again, however, it must be noted that the origins of this poetry are by no means obviously from the historical period before Muhammad; it is non-Islamic religiously (and not necessarily pre-Islamic historically), and that suggests the possibility at least that, in the period after Muhammad, vestiges of earlier religious sentiments still remained.

Of special interest is the very beginning of the book which provides a clear theological understanding of Islamic pre-history; the example illustrates well the approach of works such as these: history is presented (indeed, as one should expect) through Islamic eyes and told according to Islamic principles.

When Ishmael, son of Abraham, may God bless them both, settled in Mecca, many children were born to him such that the number of people became so numerous that they were crowded there. They displaced the original inhabitants, the Amalekites. Later on Mecca become so overcrowded that rivalries and strife arose among them, causing them to fight one another and as a result they spread out throughout the land seeking a livelihood. . . . No one left Mecca without carrying a stone from the sanctuary as a sign of veneration of it and of love for Mecca. Wherever they settled they would erect the stone and circumambulate it as they had done at the Ka'ba, thereby seeking blessing and affirming their attachment to the Ka'ba. They continued their veneration of the Ka'ba and Mecca despite this practice and still journeyed there on the pilgrimage and the visitation (*'umra*) according to the tradition inherited from Abraham and Ishmael, may God bless them both. In time this led them to worship whatever they liked. They forgot their ancient beliefs and changed the religion of Abraham and Ishmael for another. They worshipped idols and returned to the practices of the nations before them. After discovering the images which the people of Noah (on him be peace!) worshipped, they adopted the worship of those which were remembered. Among the practices were some which came down from the time of Abraham and Ishmael, including the veneration and circumambulation of the temple (in Mecca), the pilgrimage, the visitation ['umra], the standing on 'Arafa, the rituals of Muzdalifa, offering sacrifices, and uttering the ritual formulae during the pilgrimage and the visitation.[16]

The problem that such a passage is trying to solve for its readers is the following: Muslims know that the rituals connected to the Meccan pilgrimage were continuations of pre-Islamic rites; such rites had pagan connotations. How could God legitimize such activities? The answer is found in Abraham and Ishmael who, having lived in Mecca and performed the pilgrimage rites there (implicitly the same ones which Muslims perform until the present time), left the heritage of the activities, but the meaning (although not the actions themselves) of them was forgotten among the pagan inhabitants of the area. While this Abrahamic background is not appealed to in every case of a positive connection between the *jahiliyya* and Islam, it certainly is sufficiently frequent to be seen as a generalized tool for the Muslim understanding of the past. Abraham remains the 'first Muslim', putting into practice the activities which would have to be revived by Muhammad; the people in the intervening centuries are the ones who distorted the true religion which God had made available to His creation through Abraham.

The significance of pre-history

Thus we can see that the 'pre-history' of Islam is a significant concept both for historians concerned with understanding the emergence of Islam and for the Muslim community in the understanding of its relationship to its religio-cultural heritage. For the latter, the evaluation of the accomplishment of Islam in separating its faith from the past is understood in two ways, as a radical split from the past and as a continuation of the valuable (i.e. divinely sanctioned) elements. For historians the reliance on material preserved within the framework of the evaluation of the Muslim faith means that the assessment of the rise of Islam is fraught with difficulties. In the absence of assuredly contemporaneous sources, literary or epigraphical, our knowledge of 'pre-history' will remain filtered through the theologically inspired picture of the past provided by the later Muslim sources.

CHAPTER TWO

The Qur'an

It is relatively easy to give a brief description of the Qur'an in terms of the book as we have it before us today. Even the Qur'an's contents are readily summarized, as long as one does not attempt to perceive a necessarily systematic theological position within it. But accounting for how, why and when the Qur'an came into being as a text and why it looks and sounds the way it does, is far more difficult. It will be best to start with the easy tasks and then attempt the more difficult ones afterwards.

The Qur'an as a book

The Qur'an consists of 114 chapters, called *sura*s, arranged roughly in order of length from the longest (some 22 pages of Arabic text for *sura* 2) through the shortest (only a single line for *sura* 108). The major exception to this principle of ordering is the first chapter, called 'The Opening', *al-fatiha*, which is essentially a prayer and is used as such in Muslim ritual. Each chapter is divided into verses, *aya*s, the total number being figured at somewhere between 6204 and 6236, differing according to various schemes of counting. These verse divisions do not always correspond to the sense of the text but are generally related to the rhyme structure of the individual *sura*s. Twenty-nine chapters are preceded by disconnected letters of the Arabic alphabet, some single letters (Q – *qaf*, *sura* 50; N – *nun*, *sura* 68) or up to five letters together. The significance of these so-called mysterious letters has eluded traditional Muslim and modern scholarship alike. Also prefacing each chapter, with the exception of *sura* 9, is the *basmala* – the statement *In the name of God, the Mercy-giving, the Merciful*. The text as it is generally found today indicates both the Arabic consonants and the vowels according to a standard system of notation, along with a variety of other marks connected to recitation practices and verse divisions. Early manuscripts of the Qur'an dating from the eighth and ninth centuries provide only the consonantal form of the Arabic, however.

Themes of the Qur'an

Reading the Qur'an reveals that it has a thematic preoccupation with three major topics: law, the previous prophets and the final judgement. The three combine to create what has been termed by some 'a curious amalgam' of an assumption of Biblical knowledge on the part of the reader along with another element, which would appear to be some sort of native Arabian tradition.

God as the central theme

Ruling over all of the Qur'an, and the reference point for all the developments of the themes is the figure of God, Allah in Arabic. The all-mighty, all-powerful and all-merciful God has brought the world into being for the benefit of His creatures, has sent messages to them in the past to guide them in the way of living most befitting to them and to Him, has given them the law by which they should live – and which has reached its perfection and completion in Islam – and will bring about the end of the world at a time known only to Him when all shall be judged strictly according to their deeds. The basic message is a familiar one in the Judeo-Christian tradition.

The Qur'an declares in *sura* 20, verses 6–7, *No matter whether you speak out loud, He still knows your secrets and what is even more suppressed. God, there is no deity except Him! His are the Finest Names*. This emphasis on the uniqueness of God, that He is the only god who exists, is presented both in opposition to the Jewish-Christian tradition and in opposition to the polytheist idolaters.

Jews say: 'Ezra was God's son,' while Christians say: 'Christ was God's son.' That is what they say with their mouths, imitating what those have

*said who disbelieved before them. May God fight them off for what they have
trumped up! They have adopted their scholars and monks as lords instead of
God, plus Christ, the son of Mary. Yet they have been ordered to serve only
God alone; there is no deity except Him. Glory be to Him ahead of whatever
they may associate {with Him}!*

(Qur'an 9/30–1)

While the precise reference of the charge that Ezra is the son of God
according to the Jews has never been made clear, the overall emphasis of
the passage on the association of simple mortals alongside God is obvious
enough. As far as Jesus goes, there is a clear denunciation of his divine
sonship throughout the Qur'an and while he is called al-Masih, the
Messiah ('the anointed one'), this is presented as his name only and not as
an indication of his function or status.

*They have set up sprites as associates with God, even though He created
them! They have even dared to impute sons and daughters to Him without
having any knowledge. Glory be to Him; Exalted is He over whatever they
describe! Deviser of Heaven and Earth! How can He have a son while He
has no consort? He created everything and is Aware of everything! Such is
God, your Lord; there is no deity except Him, the Creator of everything, so
serve Him. He is a trustee for everything!*

(Qur'an 6/100–2)

The reference to 'sprites', the *jinn* or genies of the *Arabian Nights*, is
mentioned here in such a way as to object to their being considered as
divine powers of any sort (as apparently the polytheists thought), but
their existence is quite obviously accepted. Along with the angels and
humanity, the sprites are seen as part of creation but existing in a
different dimension. The creation of humanity from clay (Qur'an 15/26,
55/14) is paralleled by the creation of the sprites from fire (Qur'an 15/27,
55/15); the belief that the angels were created from light is a strong
tradition in Islam but it is not actually mentioned in the Qur'an.[1]
Overall, each part of creation has its own sphere and its own specific
duties in its relationship to God.

The prophets of the past

This figure of God is clearly the same God who communicated to the
prophets of the past. Qur'an 20/9–14 states:

Has Moses' story ever reached you? Once he saw a fire and told his family:

16

'Wait here; I have glimpsed a fire. Maybe I can bring you a live coal from it, or find some guidance at the fire.' As he came up to it, {a voice} called out: 'Moses, I am your Lord! Take off your sandals; you are in the sacred valley of Tuwa. I have chosen you, so listen to whatever is revealed: I am God {Alone}! There is no deity except myself, so serve Me and keep up prayer to remember Me by.'

This passage illustrates nicely the Qur'anic approach to previous revelation. The story itself is familiar from the Hebrew Bible (Exodus 3) but is presented here shorn of the extensive narrative element which seems so essential to the Judeo-Christian way of understanding its scripture. In contrast, the Qur'an simply presents a summary of the story and gets directly to the religio-moral point, each aspect of which is, in fact, central to the Islamic message: in this case, clearly, the emphasis is upon the oneness of God, but it is also on the institution of prayer and the instruction of obedience to God as the essential element of faith. To understand such passages fully in terms of a coherent overall narrative it is frequently necessary to place the Qur'anic accounts into the framework of the Biblical tradition. This fact emphasizes the need to consider an area far broader than Central Arabia when thinking of the original context of the message of Islam.

A total of twenty-eight figures besides Muhammad are named in the Qur'an as having been commissioned or selected by God to spread the message of the true way of obedience to Him. Only a limited number of these figures were given scriptures to share with the community: Adam, Abraham, Moses, David, and Jesus are specifically cited in this regard. Not all of the messengers are familiar from the Biblical tradition (or at least their identification with personages of the past is less than clear): Hud, Salih, Shu'ayb, and Luqman are generally treated as prophets of the specifically Arabian context prior to Muhammad; Dhu'l-Qarnayn is identified as Alexander the Great according to the legends which have gathered around the name and Dhu'l-Kifl, the 'Lord of the Portion' (mentioned in Qur'an 21/85 and 38/48), is variously and very uncertainly identified as Obadiah of I Kings, Ezekiel or Elijah, but is often left as 'unknown' from the perspective of history.

The stories of these prophets are recounted frequently in stereotyped passages, reflecting the general Islamic message: the prophet is commissioned by God, the prophet confronts his people, the people reject him and the people are, as a result, destroyed and the prophet and any persons faithful to his message are saved by the mercy of God. A *sura* such as the eleventh, entitled 'Hud', is typical in its presentation of these stories. Here we find, joined together in narratives always similar in structure and even in wording in some instances, accounts of Noah, Hud, Salih, Abraham, Lot, Shu'ayb, and Moses. The moral is always the same: God will triumph over the unbelievers and His message will always remain in the world in one form or another. A few other prophets have their stories told in more expansive form; the story of Joseph, recounted in *sura* 12 and one of the most cohesive narratives found in the Qur'an, is presented in a form quite full and in parts even more elaborate than the Biblical account. This elaboration indicates that the Qur'an is not simply a retelling of the Biblical stories but a reflection of their popular form in the Near Eastern milieu of the seventh century. Elements in the Qur'anic versions of these stories are sometimes found in works such as the Jewish Talmud or Midrash, for example. This indicates that the context within which the Qur'an must be read is far more than the framework provided by the text of the Bible alone; rather, the living tradition of Judaism, Christianity and all the other faiths and folklore of the area are reflected in the Qur'an and provide the necessary background for its comprehension.

The famous story from Genesis 22 of the sacrifice of the son of Abraham is also retold but the son is not identified in the Qur'an by name and his identity became, for a time, subject to great debate in Islam. The context of the Qur'anic passage would seem to suggest that Ishmael was the one who was sacrificed, since after the discussion of the sacrifice in the Qur'an (*sura* 37) the passage goes on to say *{and} We announced to him that Isaac would become a prophet who was honorable*, seeming to suggest that this was a totally separate character. The reading of Ishmael as the intended victim gained further standing through the later ideology of the Muslim community which argued that the Jews had changed the Biblical account to reflect well on their own heritage traced through Isaac; the Jews had done this rather than enhance the status of the Arabs and their descent through Ishmael (as related in the Bible, although that genealogy is nowhere echoed in the Qur'an). Regardless, the story provides another illustration of the approach of the Qur'an to Biblical narratives. Qur'an 37/101–9 states

> *When {the son} reached the stage of working alongside him, he said: 'My son, I saw in my sleep that I must sacrifice you. Look for whatever you may see {in it}.' He said: 'My father, do anything you are ordered to; you will find me to be patient, if God so wishes.' When they had both committed themselves peacefully {to God} and he placed his face down, We called out to*

him: 'Abraham, you have already confirmed the dream!' Thus We reward those who act kindly. This was an obvious test. We ransomed him by means of a splendid victim and left {him to be mentioned} among later men: 'Peace be upon Abraham!'

Compacted here into a few lines is a chapter of the Bible which has often been cited as one well crafted for its dramatic impact and use of narrative tension in having the young Isaac travelling to the sacrifice not knowing the fate in store for him. The Qur'an, however, removes the drama but saves the message, the supreme faith of both Abraham and his son; this faithful attitude on the part of Isaac is also emphasized in the development of the tradition in Jewish and then Christian circles, where in the latter instance, Abraham's son becomes the prefiguration of Jesus in his willing self-sacrifice. Also significant in the Qur'anic story is the emphasis on Abraham and his son *committing themselves*, in Arabic *aslama*, essentially *becoming Muslims*; even here then (or, perhaps, especially here), the story is told with Muslim understanding and insights.

Jesus

Similar observations can be made for the story of Jesus which, while it is found scattered throughout the Qur'an rather than in one cohesive narrative, presents a picture that has often been seen to reflect various aspects of Christianity – Gnostic, Monophysite, and Nestorian. Born of the Virgin Mary (Qur'an 19/16–29), Jesus spoke from the cradle, his first miracle. His task on earth was to provide the 'clear proofs' or 'explanations' (Qur'an 2/253 and elsewhere) and his mission was punctuated by miracles as in Qur'an 3/49: healing, knowing secrets, and fashioning birds out of clay into which he breathed life, a story known from Christian apocryphal Gospels. The crucifixion of Jesus, spoken of in Qur'an 4/157–8, has created the greatest amount of interest, with a view to its possible reflection of sectarian Christian disputes: *{The Jews} neither killed nor crucified him, even though it seemed so to them. . . . Rather God lifted him up towards Himself.* The notion that Jesus did not 'really' die on the cross has been seen as a continuation of Christian discussions over the nature of Jesus – divine and/or human. Once again, however, the Qur'an would seem to reflect a strange amalgam, on the one hand supporting the argument for the truly divine nature of Jesus and thus denying the reality of his death, while on the other hand denying that Jesus was anything other than a human being.

The message of the judgement day

All of these prophets, and many additional figures who are not mentioned by name in the Qur'an but who are said to have been sent (as Qur'an 10/47 states: *Every nation has a messenger*), brought the same message of the coming judgement for those who do not repent and follow the law of God. Qur'an 19/59–61 states:

> *Descendants {of the earlier prophets} have replaced them who neglected prayer and followed {their own} passions. They shall meet with aimlessness except for anyone who turns around (in repentance) and believes, and acts honorably; those will enter the Garden and not be harmed in any way – the gardens of Eden which the Mercy-giving has promised His servants even though {they are still} Unseen.*

The message is a simple one. All people shall die at their appointed time and then, at a point known only to God, the resurrection shall take place at which each person shall be judged according to the deeds they have performed on earth. *The agony of death will come {and confront you} with the Truth; that is what you have been trying to escape! The Trumpet shall be blown: that will be the day of the Threat!* states Qur'an 50/19–20, making reference to the eschatological trumpet, one of many Qur'anic elements familiar also from the visions of John recorded in the Book of Revelation. The scene of the judgement is painted in graphic style. For each person, a book of deeds shall be brought forth, bearing witness to his or her good or evil state (Qur'an 83); the image of the balance and the weighing of deeds is also employed (Qur'an 21/47). The judgement shall determine the ultimate fate of the individual, be that either the bliss of paradise in the Gardens or the burning torment of Hell. Both of these places are depicted in vivid terms quite frequently in the Qur'an, as for example in *sura* 55 where the *flare of sparks and fire* and the *seething bath* of Hell are contrasted to the *two gardens* of paradise which have *every kind of fruit, flowing springs*, and exotic rewards for the righteous.

The fate of the individual is described as being in the hands of God but also up to the individual. God as the all-powerful creator can control His world fully but humanity must accept responsibility for its own actions. The tension which such statements create proved to be a major topic of interest for theological speculation in Islam. But the Qur'an is clear that each individual is expected to follow the law which God has set down in His scripture, if there is to be any hope of entry into paradise in the hereafter. People are capable of sin, that being defined as an 'error' in parting from the ways of God. The figure of Satan is introduced to explain the presence of this potential for evil in the world.

The path to paradise

Qur'an 4/136 proclaims: *You who believe, believe in God and His messenger, and the Book which He has sent down to His messenger as well as the Book which He had sent down previously. Anyone who disbelieves in God and His angels, His books, His messengers and the Last Day will stray far afield.* Here is a veritable credal statement, bringing together all the elements considered essential for reaping the final reward in paradise. One must believe in the truth and the contents of the scripture; and what is the evidence of belief in it, if it is not putting the words into action? The previously quoted Qur'an 19/59–61 emphasizes the reward *for anyone who turns around (in repentance) and believes, and acts honorably.* Fulfilling the law of God – *acting honorably* – is a prerequisite for salvation of the individual. The law, as proclaimed in the Qur'an, is reminiscent of the Jewish law in matters such as its continuation of the prohibition of pork and the institution of ritual slaughter (e.g. Qur'an 2/173, 5/1–3), some purity regulations (especially regarding women, Qur'an 2/222, and within a ritual situation, Qur'an 4/43, 5/6) and the emphasis on the regulation of marriage (e.g. Qur'an 4/23), divorce (e.g. Qur'an 4/19–22), and inheritance (e.g. Qur'an 4/4–12). Clearly Islam sides with Judaism against Christianity in its position on following the law as being the appropriate implementation of faith given by God as a gift to humanity to provide guidance in living the proper, fully human life. As well, various emblems of Islam are mentioned in the Qur'an, but often only in an unelaborated form. The pilgrimage (e.g. Qur'an 2/196–200), the month of fasting (e.g. Qur'an 2/183–7), the institution of prayer (e.g. Qur'an 2/142–52, 2/238–9), and the idea of charity (e.g. Qur'an 9/53–60) are all dealt with to varying degrees; regardless of the somewhat vague nature of some of the description of these activities within the Qur'an (as compared to their elaborate formulation in other Muslim sources), it is clear that they are conceived as a compulsory part of Muslim life.

Some parallel has been seen between the Biblical 'Ten Commandments' and *sura* 17, verses 22–39.[2] Certainly the moral aim of many of the statements is similar: belief in only one God, showing respect to parents, not committing adultery and so forth. As a narrative passage, however, the law is quite clearly not presented in the same way at all in the Qur'an

21

as compared to the Bible. In no sense is this passage a pivotal or focal point of the text; nor is it portrayed in Muslim tradition as central within the context of Muhammad's career. Thus, the passage does not stand parallel to the traditional understanding of the Ten Commandments in relationship to Moses and the Bible. Rather, the law in the Qur'an is an integral part of the text with nothing to mark it off from the rest of the word of God. This presentation of the law does not preclude it being stipulated in great detail in numerous places, however, just as in the Bible:

> *Forbidden to you {in marriage} are your mothers, your {own} daughters, your sisters, your aunts on your father's side as well as aunts on your mother's side, and your brother's and your sister's daughters, your foster mothers and your foster sisters, your mothers-in-law and step-daughters who are under your guardianship {since their mothers are} wives of yours with whom you have consummated marriage (however if you have not consummated it with them, it will not be held against you) and the wives of your sons who are your own flesh-and-blood; nor may you bring two sisters together {under one roof} unless this is a thing of the past. God is Forgiving, Merciful.*

(Qur'an 4/23)

The status of the Qur'anic dispensation

The Qur'an speaks also of the law as it was revealed to the previous communities. Both the Torah of Moses and the Gospel of Jesus are specifically cited as previous revelations;[3] the Qur'an is seen as confirming both scriptures and as acting as a resolver of disputes between them: *We still sent you down the Reminder {=the Qur'an} so you may explain to mankind what was sent down to them {before}, so that they may meditate* (Qur'an 16/44). But the Qur'an also serves a correcting function because humans have misinterpreted and tampered with the earlier revelations, infusing the word of God with human perversions (see Qur'an 5/48); the Qur'an provides a clear and perfect version of the will of God, the correct rendition of revelation.

The character of the Qur'an

A summary of the contents of the Qur'an, such as that just provided, while necessarily incomplete, glosses over an important point about the composition of the book itself – its apparent random character and seemingly arbitrary sense of organization. This unique composition is illustrated by examining the contents of any of the longer *sura*s which are clearly a composite of many different themes and strata of thought. *Sura* 2, for example, the longest in the Qur'an, presents a startling picture when looked at in outline:

verses	*topic*
1–29	Faith and disbelief
30–39	Creation, Adam, Satan
40–86	Biblical history – Moses
87–103	Biblical history – Jews, Jesus, Moses
104–121	Polemic – Muslim, Jewish, Christian
122–141	Biblical history – Abraham
142–167	Islamic identity (direction of prayer, prayer itself, pilgrimage)
168–203	Juridical problems (food, wills, fast, pilgrimage, etc.)
204–214	Salvation history
215–242	Juridical problems (holy war, marriage, divorce, etc.)
243–253	Salvation history
254–260	(mixed)
261–283	Juridical problems (charity, usury)
284–286	Faith

Such a brief outline does not do justice to the complexity of the thematic structure of the *sura* by any means, but, even so, it does provide some material for provoking thought. How did the Qur'an come to look the way it does, with the subject matter within individual chapters jumping from one topic to the next, with duplications and apparent inconsistencies in grammar, law and theology abounding? To the source critic, the work displays all the tendencies of rushed editing with only the most superficial concern for the content, the editors/compilers apparently engaged only in establishing a fixed text of scripture. Within this perspective, a logical historical point for the emergence of this fixed text is provided by the rise of the Qur'an to a status of absolute authority in matters of law and theology (as compared to the authority of tradition, of the caliph or of reason). Creating a stable text of scripture, canonizing the various elements into a whole, may be seen as going hand-in-hand with the text being confirmed as the major source of legal and theological authority for the Muslim community.

Muslim accounts of the collection of the text

Of course, the Muslim community itself has an explanation for why the Qur'an looks the way it does, but the contradictory nature of the accounts within the multiplicity of different versions of the story has raised grave doubts on the part of many scholars as to their motivation. Generally, Muhammad himself is excluded from any role in the collection of the text, although it is possible to find some accounts which talk of him going over the whole text with 'Ali, his cousin, son-in-law and figurehead of the later Shi'ite group. Zayd ibn Thabit, a companion of Muhammad, is generally credited with an early collection of the scripture and the pages of the text are said to have been entrusted to Hafsa, one of Muhammad's wives. Under the instructions of 'Uthman, the third ruler of the empire after the death of Muhammad, the major collection of the text 'as we now have it' is said to have taken place. Working on the basis of pieces of text written 'on palm leaves or flat stones or in the hearts of men', the complete text (deemed to have survived in full) was written out in full and distributed to the major centres of the early empire. Thus, within thirty years of the death of Muhammad, it is understood that the Qur'an existed in at least its skeleton but fixed form; theologically, it is held that the form that the text was in at this point was an image of the 'heavenly tablet', suggesting that its form and content were precisely that which God desired for it.[4] From this skeleton text, which indicated only the consonants of the Arabic script in a rudimentary form, the final text of the Qur'an was developed over the next two centuries, such that all the subtleties of the language and the script were indicated. It is held that an oral tradition preserved the full text from the time of its revelation, the written form serving only as a mnemonic device for memorization of the text.

The authority of the Qur'an

The value and the point of such stories is still under debate among scholars but, whatever the case, one thing remains quite clear. The Qur'an is, and has been from the beginning of the emergence of Islam as a religion, the primary source and reference point. Indeed, the Qur'an in its function as that source of authority is the defining point of Islamic identity. The emergence of the Muslim community is intimately connected with the emergence of the Qur'an as an authoritative text in making decisions on matters of law and theology. What research has revealed is that the scripture's status and authority was debated in early times, especially between the various religious communities of the Near East and also within the newly-emerging Islamic community itself. Elements of the process by which the Qur'an emerged as the authoritative source, side-by-side with the emergence of the community of Islam itself, can be traced in the writing of various texts of Qur'anic interpretation in the early centuries of Islam,[5] in early works of law, and in several documents of inter-religious polemic. The ultimate enshrinement of the text of the Qur'an as we now know it, understood to be literally the word of God and thereby having its authority within the community, was the result of two to three centuries of vigorous debate, as reflected in these texts.

Theology and the Qur'an

Supporting the status of the authority of the Qur'an are a number of theological dogmas connected directly to the book by which institutionalized Islam was able to argue for the Qur'an as the prime source in law and theology. These dogmas have as their end result the skirting of issues connected to the construction of the text by seeing the very shape of the book as evidence of the divine hand at work. But it is on this point that early polemical texts reveal a great deal of discussion and early Islamic exegetical texts dealing with the Qur'an indicate that the argument concerning the form of the text as evidence of divine authorship took at least three centuries to reach its fully developed form.

The Qur'an as the proof of Islam

It would appear that, early on, Muslims had to defend their nascent religion against Christian theological attack in the area of the Fertile Crescent, especially Iraq. The following argument was constructed: miracles prove the status of prophethood and the Qur'an is Muhammad's miracle; therefore, Muhammad was truly a prophet and Islam is a true, revealed religion. All participants in the debate appear to have agreed on the first premise. What Muslims had to prove, and Christians disprove, was the validity of the second, for the conclusion, the truth of Islam, stood or fell on its credibility. Over time, the argument became one concerned to prove the 'inimitability' of the Qur'an, an argument which, its proponents were quick to point out, had a basis in the Qur'an itself, although whether that was clear before the demands of the argument were put upon those verses is not entirely obvious. Known as the 'challenge verses', the production of a text 'like' the Qur'an is encouraged but known to be impossible: *Produce a chapter like it* [i.e. the Qur'an], *or appeal to anyone you can manage to besides God if you are so truthful* (Qur'an 10/38); *Well then bring (ten) chapters made up like it!* (Qur'an 11/13). God has given the Qur'an to Muhammad and because of its divine origin, no text 'like' it can, in fact, be produced. The inimitability of the text proves its divine authorship and thus its status as a miracle, confirming Muhammad's role and the veracity of Islam.

Polemical texts from some 150–200 years after Muhammad indicate the sorts of discussions that were going on; the existence of the arguments indicates that there were no clearly formulated Muslim answers to these concerns at the time. That suggests that the Qur'an as a fixed text of scripture was still in the process of finding support for its authority within the community; indeed, it took at least a hundred more years before the full enunciation of the doctrine of inimitability could respond cohesively to such challenges. The Christian al-Kindi, who wrote a text around the year 830, starts off by demanding the following: 'Show me any proof or sign of a wonderful work done by your master Muhammad, to certify his mission, and to prove what he did in slaughter and rapine was, like the other, by Divine command.' The isolation of one of the central elements of Christian polemic against Islam – that Muhammad's religion was spread by the sword – is combined here with the demand for proof of a miracle. Anticipating the Muslim response that the Qur'an was that evidence, al-Kindi continues:

> The result of all of this [process by which the Qur'an came into being] is patent to you who have read the scriptures and see how, in your book, histories are all jumbled together and intermingled; an evidence that many different hands have been at work therein, and caused discrepancies, adding or cutting out whatever they liked or disliked. Are such, now, the conditions of a revelation sent down from heaven?[6]

The literary state of the Qur'an is used against the Muslims by al-Kindi as proof of its non-divine origin.

The doctrine of inimitability

The Muslim response to these charges did not reach its full defensive literary expression until towards the end of the tenth century in the hands of the theologian-grammarian al-Rummani (d. 996) who argued for the *i'jaz*, 'inimitability', of the Qur'an on the basis primarily of its literary qualities, especially its easily quantifiable merits such as its conciseness.[7] At one point in his argument, he cites a popular Arab saying and suggests that its meaning is close to a Qur'anic statement but then points out that the Qur'an expresses the same sentiment (and even more, he claims) in fewer letters. Furthermore, what to polemical writers of earlier centuries were faults within the Qur'an – evidence of its human production and thus non-miraculous status – become for al-Rummani positive elements within the book; ellipses within the text, for example, are considered positive rhetorical devices rather than evidence of rushed or sloppy writing. Much of this sort of argumentation becomes tied to an understanding of the nature of the Arabic language, a language full of rhetorical potential of which, naturally, the Qur'an must take full advantage. The Qur'an, according to its own statements (Qur'an 12/2, 26/192–5) has been revealed by God *in a clear Arabic tongue* and, the argument is made, must partake in all the features of that language. This sort of argument is difficult, if not impossible, to evaluate, due to the lack of contemporaneous profane literature by which the rhetorical accomplishment of the Qur'an can actually be assessed; the argument remains a dogmatic one, essential to the proof of the status of the text, but one which operates (like many other religious arguments) within the presuppositions of Islam alone.

Interpretation of the Qur'an

In fact, Muslims, in the two centuries for which there is some literary evidence before al-Rummani, appear to have had slightly different feelings about their scripture. They appear to have been more concerned with cataloguing the peculiarities of the text themselves and facing the practical job of understanding the text, rather than worrying about defending its intricacies. That is, the more general problem of interpretation, and hand-in-hand with that, the consolidation of its authority through clear enunciation of its meaning, was of far greater concern.

The text of the Qur'an presents many ambiguities, difficult words whose precise readings are unsure, problems of textual division and apparently incompatible statements. With the text's rise to the status of authority, or perhaps parallel to it and stimulating that very rise to authority, there emerged the discipline of interpretation, known as *tafsir* or, in a more general sense, the Qur'anic sciences called *'ulum al-Qur'an*. One work by Abu 'Ubayda (who died in 824), for example, presents a listing of types of 'problematic' verses in the Qur'an and their explanation; items such as ellipses due to omission, grammatical discord (e.g. plural verbs with singular subjects) and variation in the treatment of the gender of nouns are all recorded. This process of cataloguing difficulties in the Qur'an is also found in other works treating the vocabulary of the text itself as well as its stylistic features and variant readings. With the emergence of the doctrine of inimitability, the attitude towards these sorts of elements changed, as has been suggested. More major works of interpretation of the Qur'an emerged late in the ninth century, and they aimed to clarify the text in light of contemporary understandings and conditions. Not only was this the result of the maturation of the Muslim community and a consolidation of opinion about the scripture but it was also the result of practical pressures. As the Islamic community expanded, it embraced a large number of people who did not know Arabic and who were not fully acquainted with the Biblical tradition, which, as was pointed out earlier, seems to be an assumed basis for understanding the Qur'anic text. The first landmark of what became a vast library of books providing comprehensive interpretations of the Qur'an, was written by Abu Ja'far al-Tabari who died in 923.[8] A verse-by-verse analysis provides a detailed discussion of every major interpretational trend (except sectarian tendencies, for example Shi'ite); every idea is documented by the transmission of the opinions said to derive from Muhammad or his closest companions, who are naturally pictured as having the best information regarding understanding the text.

The Qur'an as an object of faith

For the Muslim community, the Qur'an is the word of God as revealed to Muhammad, the focal point of the Islamic faith. As a symbol of that faith, the book has naturally garnered far more importance for the individual believer than the polemical discussions just sketched would suggest. After all, for Muslims there is no doubt about the status of their scripture; at every moment, their faith confirms for them the rightness of the book. There arose a great number of beliefs about the text of the book itself, separate from its contents, which reflect the honour and significance which is accorded to the scripture as a book. Within at most two hundred years of the death of Muhammad, traditions arose speaking of the significance of individual sections of the Qur'an. The first chapter, *surat al-fatiha*, is not only argued to be an essential element of the ritual of prayer,[9] but also the 'greatest' of all the *sura*s, the recitation of which is recorded as curing the bite of a scorpion, for example; likewise, *sura*s 113 and 114 are seen as effective in curing illnesses. Reciting specific individual portions of the Qur'an, the last two verses of *sura* 2 especially, are spoken of as giving protection from Satan for the night. Recitation of *sura* 18, *sura* 48, or *sura* 112 brings merit and benefits.[10] The result of these practices has been the emergence of a complex group of medical and spiritual beliefs all connected to the book, known as *khawass al-Qur'an*. The history of these practices, like most popular beliefs, is not well known but it is likely that modern practices,[11] such as wearing a tiny copy of the Qur'an or the name Allah as an amulet, in the manner in which Christians wear a crucifix or Jews a star of David, have a heritage which extends well back into the early Islamic period. The Qur'an has been the central symbol of Islam as well as its vital source and, as is true of Jesus in Christianity, its power and effect to move and motivate individuals has never been underestimated by Muslims.

CHAPTER THREE

Muhammad

The problem of Muhammad's biography

Unlike certain famous instances in the modern study of Jesus in Christianity, contemporary scholarship on Islam has generally not seen fit to postulate that Muhammad did not exist. That someone named Muhammad embodied the rallying point for the Arab conquests and provided the tag for a religious doctrine in the name of which the conquered lands were united, there really is little doubt; at the very least, no profit is to be gained from denying those facts in terms of providing a cohesive historical picture. Sources external to the nascent Islamic society itself provide evidence, albeit somewhat at variance with the 'accepted' portrait of the Arabian prophet, that confirms the role of the figure himself. These sources are limited in number, extremely hard to date (raising questions of Muslim influence upon the writers, if the source is, in fact, much later than claimed) and questionable in their supposed 'disinterested' or 'objective' presentation of history.[1]

Despite the existence of these external sources and the proliferation of documentation from within the community, the fact of the matter remains that it is very difficult to talk about Muhammad, in either his political or religious guise, free from the perspective which later Muslim tradition has imposed upon him. The biography of Muhammad has served a number of important functions in Islam, each of which has coloured it in crucial ways. There are two major aspects which must be confronted here. One, Muhammad's biography must be understood as a framework for the revelation of the Qur'an, and two, it must be understood as a source for the normative example, *sunna*, of Muhammad.

Muslim sources for the life of Muhammad

Material on the life of Muhammad is available in ample if not in fact excessive quantities. The earliest complete extant text stems from a version of the biography (*Sira*) of Muhammad by Ibn Ishaq (d. 767) edited by Ibn Hisham (d. 833). This may be supplemented by other fairly early texts such as those by al-Waqidi (d. 823) and Ibn Sa'd (d. 845). Also useful are the later *hadith* collections which gather together anecdotes about Muhammad and his life, generally organized according to legal topics and communicated by Muhammad's closest followers, his so-called 'companions'. In broad outline, all these sources present the same story but matters of chronology and detail are always problematic.

The account of the events during Muhammad's life is fairly standardized, despite the multiplicity of sources available and the numerous disagreements among scholars of Islam as to how to interpret the material in a meaningful way. Most accounts go back to the text of Ibn Ishaq, supplemented by the various other sources. Despite valiant attempts by some scholars to elicit information, the Qur'an has proven very opaque when it comes to Muhammad: the name is mentioned four times – Qur'an 3/144, 33/40, 47/2, 48/29 – but without prior knowledge of the *Sira* accounts of Ibn Ishaq, the material provides no data beyond asserting Muhammad's existence and a conception of his prophetic role; furthermore, since in many places the *Sira* may well be attempting to explain, make sense of, or clarify the elliptical and allusive text of the Qur'an, there is the danger of going around in interpretative circles. The absence of biographical material is but one example of a general tendency in the Qur'an not to provide any overall context. The Qur'an simply does not provide the necessary clarifying keys by which it would be possible to extract data concerning the contemporary Arabian context, beyond the citation of a few names.[2] It is in this vein, then, that one of the roles of the biography of Muhammad in Islam is to be understood as providing the contextual framework for the revelation of the Qur'an. While the details of this framework are frequently vague and contradictory, the basic theological point stands, underpinning the entire biographical corpus: God has revealed the Qur'an to Muhammad, an ordinary man living among the Arab tribes, over a twenty-two-year period.[3] As a result, the entire biographical account has been coloured by these efforts to situate and interpret the Qur'an.

The life of Muhammad in the sources

Muhammad is said to have been born around 570; this is a date fixed by a tradition which records that the 'Expedition of the Elephant', the expedition by a ruler of south Arabia named Abraha, into the homeland of Muhammad, the Hijaz, was in the same year. The evidence for the date of the expedition being 570 is undermined by inscriptional material found in south Arabia, which makes it more likely to have been at the end of the 540s. The significance of the date in the Muslim context is that it serves to establish Muhammad's age as forty when he started to receive revelations, the number forty being one of general spiritual significance in the Near East region.[4]

Muhammad was born into the family of Banu Hashim in the tribe of Quraysh; his family was a prominent but not dominant group in the society at the time. He was orphaned at an early age, and lived a meagre existence until he married Khadija, an older woman with substantial financial involvement with the camel-caravan trade. Muhammad is thought to have been involved in the trade himself. At the age of forty he is said to have gone on a solitary retreat in the hills near Mecca, following a religious practice of the time, at which point the angel Gabriel came to him to inform him of his commission as a prophet of the one God, Allah. To this event is traditionally connected the Qur'anic passage contained in *sura* 96: *Read in the name of your Lord Who creates, creates man from a clot! Read, for your Lord is most Generous; {it is He} Who teaches by means of the pen, teaches man what he does not know.* Stories of self-doubt are connected with this call to prophethood but eventually Muhammad followed his orders and preached the message of the Qur'an. He had little success to begin with, perhaps converting some of the lower class members of his society, along with his wife Khadija and 'Ali, his cousin, future son-in-law, fourth Caliph and figurehead of the Shi'ite movement in Islam. As Muhammad hardened his attack on the polytheistic society of Mecca, its inequalities and hypocrisies, the inhabitants became more resentful of his presence. It has been speculated that the cause of some of this resentment was his attack upon the institutions of the Meccan society, especially the town's connection to the religious shrine, the Ka'ba, which gave it a degree of prominence in Arabia at the time. Persecution of the members of this new religion is said to have increased substantially, and traditions tell of a group of believers who emigrated to Abyssinia, perhaps going there to find asylum among the Christians or to attempt to make more converts among an audience who may have been thought to be sympathetic to the message of the movement. Meanwhile, Muhammad made efforts to find a new place to live in Arabia, trying the neighbouring town of al-Ta'if, before being invited to Yathrib (later to be called Medina, or fully, Medinat al-nabi, the 'City of the prophet') some 400 kilometres northeast of Mecca. Communities of Jews were living in Yathrib and these people are suggested to have been part of the attraction of the location, for a sympathetic audience for the message of Muhammad was anticipated among these 'people of the book'.

The move to Yathrib is referred to as the *hijra* ('emigration' or 'flight') and the year in which it happened (622) serves as the focal point of the Muslim calendar. An event to which the Qur'an provides only ambiguous reference, it is regardless seen as the time at which the Muslim community came into being and thus the appropriate starting point for calendar dating (the notion of 'community', *umma*, being a defining point of the Islamic sense of identity). There do not appear to be any instances of the mention of the idea of a *hijri* calendar in coins or documents from the seventh century; rather, an undefined era is employed or reference is made to an era (apparently starting in 622 CE, however) as the 'rule of the Arabs'.[5] Defining the calendar in terms of the *hijra* appears to be linked with the rise of Islam as a state religion, a notion to be explored further in the next chapter.

It was in Yathrib/Medina that Muhammad emerged as a forceful religious and political leader, leading the Medinan community under the terms of a type of treaty, the so-called 'Constitution of Medina', within which his authority was said ultimately to derive from God: the ideal religio-political aspects of Muslim community life are embodied here. Controlled in this 'constitution' were the political and civil relations of the various tribes within the Medinan federation, with all disputes to be brought before Muhammad for arbitration. The 'constitution' explicitly states:

> Whenever a dispute or controversy likely to cause trouble arises among the people of this document, it shall be referred to God and to Muhammad, the apostle of God. God is the guarantor of the pious observance of what is in this document.[6]

The actual conversion of the inhabitants of Medina to Islam was not immediate and the Jewish communities were accused of treachery and, eventually, all were either removed or attacked.

Muhammad's strategy in Medina, especially after his realization that the Jews were not the ready audience for his message which he had anticipated, was to return to Mecca. This aim was pursued through an attempt to curtail the trade of Mecca by random attacks on the camel caravans, producing unstable conditions for reliable conduct of business as well as bringing the profits of such raids into Medinan hands, thus producing power and prestige for the community in the eyes of the Arabian tribes.[7] The most important of these raids was known as the battle of Badr; taking place in 624, it started as an attack on a Meccan caravan and then became a battle with the Meccan Quraysh tribe. It provided a great victory for Muhammad and his followers, a victory which was taken as a sign of divine pleasure with the strategy. The year 625 saw an attack by the Quraysh in the Battle of Uhud, resulting in a defeat for Muhammad's followers, while in 627, a Meccan army laid seige to Medina in the Battle of the Ditch. The Medinans were able to withstand the onslaught, however, and the Meccans were forced to withdraw after 40 days. This success was followed by an attack directly on Mecca led by Muhammad, which ended not with a battle but with the Treaty of Hudaybiya, the terms of which allowed the Medinans to enter Mecca the next year in order to perform the pilgrimage; that treaty was honoured. By that time, the power of the Medinan community had grown by great strides in Arabia and, by the next year, 630, Muhammad was able to attack and take over Mecca, meeting little resistance to his efforts. The final two years of Muhammad's life were spent in Mecca, with him attempting to consolidate his position in Arabia with alliances, and at least nominal conversion to Islam, of the nomadic bedouin of Arabia.

Difficulties with the biography

This is the basic account of the life of Muhammad as it is presented in the narrative sources available to us. Many aspects of it are debatable, especially in matters of precise dating and, on that basis alone, the summary of the 'life of Muhammad' as presented here is fraught with difficulties and insoluble problems. Evidence of such things as the sources' tendency to 'improve' over time – such that later sources are able to provide specific data when earlier ones are vague – and the overt intention of much of the material to interpret unclear passages of the Qur'an as mentioned above, suggests that texts such as Ibn Ishaq's *Sira* are far more complex in literary terms than a historical biography might popularly be conceived today. Essentially, these texts were involved in creative story-telling where the manifestation of the raconteur's ability to elaborate, entertain and enhance were highly praised merits. Underlying the whole structure, however, is the attempt to provide a context for the revelation of the Qur'an, such that ambiguous references may be made clear through the process of interpretation.

The mythic dimension of Muhammad's biography

One other related factor acts to restrict the amount of confidence that may be placed in these accounts of Muhammad's life, even disregarding disputes over small details. The religious importance of Muhammad is such that it is not really feasible (nor necessarily desirable) to distinguish later religiously-inspired fiction from what might be called historical 'fact'. The entire structure of a work such as that of Ibn Ishaq suggests that many elements are constructed from what have been termed by one scholar 'mythic topoi', or basic religious narrative and thematic conventions. Such topoi were employed throughout the Near Eastern area in the construction of literary lives of religious figures. In addition, the *Sira* text is composed of lists, documents, genealogies, chronologies, poetry, and formal prose.[8] The overall effect is to create a picture of both Muhammad and the Muslim community in its 'pristine' form; this means that the picture which emerges, and the impulse behind its composition, is a normative one – this is a picture of how the Muslim community should be, projected back into the times of its founder who has been described in mythic terms. Its intention is to portray the religion of Islam as conceptually identifiable from the time of Muhammad.

A part of the reason for having produced such a picture of Muhammad was to create an expression of Islam which separated it clearly from Judaism and Christianity: this is the theme of the second part of this book. The role of the figurehead of a religion in producing identity for the religious community is evident in all three of the monotheistic traditions and Muhammad's place in this inter-religious rivalry was established through both the Qur'an (as the book given specifically to him, as the oral and written Torahs were revealed to Moses) and through the biographical material. The major concern displayed through a work such as Ibn Ishaq's *Sira* is the acceptance or rejection by various groups of the credentials in the hands of the messenger, that is the scripture. At stake, then, is the authority of the person of Muhammad, not in terms of law but as a prophet. The connection of Muhammad to the revelation of the Qur'an then becomes central.[9]

The significance of the figure of Muhammad

Another reason for the emergence of this elaborated, detailed picture of Muhammad is far more complex and vital to the enterprise of Islam itself. In fact, regardless of how interesting the events of Muhammad's life may be, the significance for Muslims of the person himself and the actual 'facts' of the narrative (as opposed to its overall theological point) does not lie particularly in the historical narrative at all. Rather, it is the anecdotes about his life, the *hadith*, and the more generalized aspects of what that behaviour represents, that concerns the community most of all: this is the *sunna*, the 'example' provided by the life of Muhammad which every Muslim attempts to emulate. Of course, the two aspects — the historical and the anecdotal — are intertwined and, for the historian, indistinguishable; this is, as a consequence, what has created some of the problems in trying to reconstruct the 'historical Muhammad'.

The material of tradition

The information which is found in works such as that of Ibn Ishaq (at least in germ form) and which has been gathered together into the works of *hadith* especially, is believed by Muslims to have been transmitted from the earliest generations of community members down to the collectors of these books. Such transmissions are documented by what is known as the *isnad*, the 'chain' of transmitters of a report (listed backwards chronologically), while the actual text is known as the *matn*. An example is the following:

> Ishaq told me that 'Ubayd Allah told him on the authority of Shayban on the authority of Yahya on the authority of Muhammad ibn 'Abd al-Rahman, client of Banu Zuhra, on the authority of Abu Salama on the authority of 'Abd Allah ibn 'Umar that he said, 'The messenger of God (may the prayers and peace of God be upon him) said to me, "Recite all of the Qur'an in one month". I said, "But I am able to do more than that!" So (Muhammad) said, "Then recite it in seven days, but do not do it in less than that".'[10]

Reports such as these comprise the text of a series of books devoted to the gathering together of the material, which may be arranged either according to the transmitter of the report or according to the legal topic.

This latter method of organization proved the most successful, it being the principle employed in the six works which are accepted as being of major importance by the majority of Muslims; these books collect together what were considered genuine *hadith* reports (and, as such, the reports serve as the theoretical basis for Islamic law). The books were compiled by al-Bukhari (d. 870), Muslim ibn al-Hajjaj (d. 875), Ibn Maja (d. 887), Abu Dawud (d. 889), al-Tirmidhi (d. 892) and al-Nasa'i (d. 915) respectively.

All the reports in these books deal with what Muhammad said and did, and of what he approved or disapproved implicitly (as indicated by his general behaviour). They are classified into subjects which would appear to follow the legal discussion taking place at the time of their compilation. Al-Bukhari, for example, has a total of 93 chapters with headings but in some chapters there are in fact no *hadith* reports to be found; it is clear, therefore, that he was working with a pre-arranged structure and was attempting to document the issues under discussion. The chapter headings do, however, reflect the concerns of Muslim life, ones which go beyond any narrow definition of 'law' and encompass many different aspects. To take al-Bukhari as an example again, his work starts with what might be considered 'theological' topics: revelation, faith, and knowledge. He then deals with various aspects of prayer (chapters 4 to 23), followed by charity, pilgrimage, and fasting (chapters 24 to 32). Covered there are what have become the central symbols of Islam, enshrined in the concept of the 'five pillars' (see chapter 7 below). After that the book covers, in chapters 33 to 53, general interactions between people (with special emphasis on commerce), and then turns to certain religious concepts such as the merit of the prophets and the Qur'an. Marriage and divorce follow, then a wide variety of topics, ranging from medicine and good manners to apostasy and dreams. The work finishes with 'The Unity of God', thus bringing the sequence to closure. Muhammad, therefore, is conceived to have had some bearing on all aspects of Muslim life, both the personal and the interpersonal, as reflected in this categorization of the *hadith* material.

The problem of hadith reports

For an individual report itself, the *isnad*, or chain of transmitters, is considered to act as a guarantor of the genuineness of the text of the report. However, the *isnad* mechanism was, according to Muslims, subject to a great deal of fraud in the early period. Muslims therefore created several methods of evaluating these *isnad*s, using criteria which dealt in particular with the life and character of the individual transmitters found in the sequence of names. The desire was to document *isnad*s which were complete in their testimony to the transmission of the text of the report from generation to generation; the citation of people of high moral integrity who conceivably could have met in their lifetimes so that the reports could have been passed on physically was the important factor in the assessment of the chains of transmitters. Not surprisingly perhaps, such methods could really only sort out the inept *isnad* fabrications from the less inept. Thus we find in the collections of *hadith* materials, reports which clearly are concerned with matters of interest to the community in generations after Muhammad but which have been framed as predictions made by him. An example is the following, which raises the divisive issue of free will versus predestination as discussed by theologians several centuries into the Islamic era:

> Bundak told us that 'Abd al-Rahman ibn Mahdi told him that Shu'ba told him on the authority of 'Asim ibn 'Abd Allah who said that he heard Salim ibn 'Abd Allah reporting on the authority of his father who said that 'Umar said: 'O messenger of God, what do you think? Are the works which we do of our own creation or are they settled in advance by God?' (Muhammad) said: 'They are indeed settled in advance, O Ibn al-Khattab, and everything has been made easy [see Qur'an 80/20]. Whoever is of the people of happiness will do that which leads to happiness, and whoever is of the people of misery will do that which leads to misery.'[11]

Here Muhammad is employed as a spokesperson for the theological party which supported the doctrine of predestination; in that way, those people tried to assert the rightness of their position by citing Muhammad as their proof. *Hadith* reports may also be found which also support the opposite position.

It has also been discovered by modern researchers that *isnad*s had a tendency to 'grow backwards'. In certain early texts a statement will be found attributed to a caliph of the Umayyad dynasty, for example, or will even be unattributed, as in the case of certain legal maxims; elsewhere, the same statements will be found in the form of *hadith* reports with fully documented *isnad*s going back to Muhammad or one of his companions. There are instances where it would have been appropriate on the basis of the arguments being conducted in texts to cite the given report from Muhammad, had such reports been available; but, in fact, unattributed statements are found. The conclusion to be drawn from this is that at a certain point in time the *isnad* had not yet been fully developed and was not yet considered by some authors necessary to establish a report's authority. Only when the significance of a given statement was fully established did the *isnad* 'grow backwards' to include Muhammad and thus invest an opinion with the authority of the prophet of Islam.[12]

The authority of Muhammad

This fabrication of *hadith* reports arose because of the importance which Muslims attributed to Muhammad in the elaboration of Islam. Muhammad's example became the legal basis for substantiation of individual items of Muslim behaviour. As we shall see in chapter six on the development of law, Muhammad's practice or *sunna* became a source of law in Islam (second only to the Qur'an) as a result of the desire to introduce both some uniformity and a sense of defined authority into the Muslim community. Because of this, the name and the authority of Muhammad were used to substantiate legal positions; what a given group of Muslims felt was the correct or appropriate legal practice would at the same time be felt to be (undoubtedly quite sincerely) the practice of Muhammad.

The crucial question, which is much debated in modern scholarship, is when did Muhammad emerge as being the source of authority for the community, which is clearly the position attributed to him by the ninth century?

Certainly the status of the authority of Muhammad in the early Muslim community is not clear. Coins which refer to him as *rasul Allah*, the 'messenger of God', start appearing only in the 60s and 70s of the *hijri* calendar and even then such citations need not be taken as necessarily invoking his authority; rather, his symbolic value as an emblem of Islam — a part of an emerging self-definition — would appear to be the point of such references, since the caliph was at the same time proclaiming himself the authority in the living community as the *khalifat Allah* (a matter discussed in chapter 4 below). This same question also arises in the context of the discussion of the law as to when the notion of the 'local tradition' as being the basis of legal practice was supplanted by the *sunna* or guided practice of Muhammad specifically as second only to the Qur'an.

Clearly then, the status of Muhammad as the legal grounding for the community's actions and beliefs had an impact on the biographical material which is available to us today. Much of the material tells us more about the developments within the later Muslim community – the issues which were being elaborated, the debates which were going on – than it does about Muhammad as a person. All the material is of great value to the historian, therefore, but it must be treated with a discerning, critical eye, always alert to the ideological value contained within any reminiscence or anecdote.

The significance of Muhammad

In sum, then, the life of Muhammad may be recounted on the basis of various sources and its details may be debated. The value of it as a grounding for the Qur'an may be examined. The development of Muhammad's role as an authority in the community can be analysed and evidence cited. All such discussion, however, misses the essence of Muslim feelings about the significance of Muhammad.

It has often been commented that while Muslims may think those who deny the existence of God or who utter blasphemies about Him are misguided, such discussions will not offend in the same manner in which discussions over Muhammad will. Those who insinuate evil of Muhammad or who cast aspersions on him are considered to be insulting Islam. This, upon consideration, is not surprising. The charges laid by Christians against Islam in medieval times always focused on Muhammad and his use of 'holy war', *jihad*, the permission of polygamy and the number of marriages consummated by Muhammad himself. 'Insulting' Muhammad in any way, therefore, always recreates the image of those times and raises the suspicion that such charges are being laid once again, even if they are in different words. But further thought reveals that 'attacking' Muhammad is, of course, attacking the way of life of individual Muslims, for their way of life is understood to rest on the example of the founder of their religion. If something is felt by Muslims to be a denigration of one aspect of the life of Muhammad then by implication such may be seen as an attack on the whole way of life of each and every Muslim, at least in its idealized conception.

Muhammad as exemplar

Muhammad, as is implied in the basis of the entire concept of the *sunna*, is the 'perfect man'. He is the most liberal, the best, the bravest. Most of all, Muhammad is considered to have lived his life in a state of sinlessness (*isma'*); with such a doctrine, everything Muhammad did is considered to be the perfect embodiment of the will of God – nothing at any point of his life would have been in contravention of that will. This is a doctrine which took a number of centuries to become firmly established in Islam, as evidenced by some early, divergent material which seems to present Muhammad as capable of making mistakes, even on very basic religious issues.[13] It is quite likely that the significance of the doctrine should be viewed in tandem with that of the *i'jaz*, 'inimitability', of the Qur'an; Muhammad's sinlessness not only protects the concept of the *sunna* but also the contents of the Qur'an from any lack of perfection.

Elaborations of the mythic portrait of Muhammad

The picture of Muhammad has, as a result of the notion of sinlessness, been subject to all sorts of 'fantastic' elaborations, creating a mythic image of the prophet of Islam. A portrait of the 'perfect man' emerges, providing details even of his physical description:

> [Muhammad's hair was] neither lank nor short and woolly. It touched his shoulders. Muhammad used to make four plaits with each ear exposed between two plaits. The number of white hairs did not exceed seventeen. His eyes were very wide and black. His nose was hooked. He had a broad chest. Between his navel and upper chest there was a single hair. He had three belly folds.[14]

Descriptions such as these are not abundant in Muslim texts but they do display at least one aspect of the devotion to Muhammad who, although he is only ever said to have been an ordinary mortal with no supernatural attributes, inevitably became the focus for much popular speculation.

The night journey of Muhammad

More prominent in this elaboration of the picture of Muhammad is the story of his night journey (*isra'*) to Jerusalem and his ascension into heaven (*mi'raj*). Not only is the narrative a favourite in and by itself, but the stories have been the subject of numerous artistic endeavours.[15] The story also provides at least some of the sanction for the significance of Jerusalem in Muslim piety (this is the place from which Muhammad ascended into heaven); the account of the ascension stands as a model of Muslim spiritual devotion when interpreted on a metaphorical level as the inner journey leading to the vision of God. Issues dealing with the nature of heaven and hell, their existence and the conditions for entrance often find themselves attached to this story. Finally, the stipulation of five prayers a day as the requirement for Muslims also finds its support in the narrative. The story functions on many different levels, therefore, and is not only a vehicle for flights of popular imagination.

Traditionally pegged to Qur'an 17/1, *Glory be to Him, Who had His servant travel by night from the Hallowed Mosque to the Further Mosque whose surroundings We have blessed, so that We might show him some of Our signs! He is the Alert, the Observant!*, the story tells of Muhammad travelling to Jerusalem on the back of the winged horse Buraq and from there ascending through the seven levels of heaven, meeting the great prophets of the past as he progresses: Adam, John, Jesus, Joseph, Enoch, Aaron, Moses, and Abraham. He is given a view of various aspects of hell as well. Finally he is allowed a vision of God and is given the command of fifty prayers a day for his followers. In a narrative reminiscent of the Sodom and Gomorrah account in Genesis 18, Muhammad, at Moses's insistence, returns to God to bargain for a lower requirement; the final result is the five daily prayers. Muhammad returns to Mecca and tells of his adventure and is able to prove the veracity of his story by knowing of the imminent arrival of a caravan in his home town which he saw when returning on Buraq. The proof of the mission provides a rousing climax to the account. When asked what proof he had for his journey to Jerusalem, Muhammad replied that:

he had passed a certain caravan in a certain valley and the animal which he was riding on scared them and a camel ran away. [He said], 'I showed them where it was while on my way to al-Shams. I carried on until I reached Dajanan where I passed by another caravan. The people were sleeping; they had a jar of water which was covered with something. I uncovered it, drank some water and replaced the cover as I had found it. The evidence of this is that their caravan is now approaching from al-Bayda at the pass of al-Tan'im; it is led by a dark-coloured camel with two sacks on it, one black, the other multi-coloured.' The people hurried to the pass and it was as Muhammad had described.[16]

The basic substance of the entire story of the night journey and ascension is found in Ibn Ishaq's *Sira* and it has continued to be elaborated up until today.[17] Such imaginative stories are not abundant in the life account of Muhammad (as compared to Jesus's for example) but they do tend to play an important role both in providing a guarantee of

Muhammad's status and in supplying a focal point for popular belief. Other instances of folk stories are frequently connected to Muhammad's birth and youth. Very popular is the account of angels visiting him to cleanse his heart. The story exists in many renditions but all include the basic elements of two men in white clothes seizing the infant Muhammad, opening his chest and removing his heart. They then proceed to wash his heart in a golden basin with purifying water from the well of Zamzam which was located next to the Ka'ba in Mecca. This type of story and many others like it reveal a colorful adaptation of Jewish and Christian legends regarding prophetic qualifications and initiation; the stories frequently combine this thematic borrowing with anecdotes spun around statements from the Qur'an, as in the instance of the account of the heavenly journey.[18]

Muhammad as intecessor

Another aspect of the popular Muhammad is of great significance and that is his role as intercessor on behalf of the members of his community on the day of judgement. While not finding any explicit support within the Qur'an (which emphasizes individual responsibility on this point), it is commonly held that Muhammad will act as an advocate before God on behalf of his people. While this sort of idea has not developed into a notion of redemption through the prophet by his suffering on other's behalf, as in Christianity, nor into an idea of Muhammad having some sort of store of merit which he can share, his role is clearly enunciated in the texts of classical Islam which concentrate on the events on the day of judgement. A text ascribed to the famous Sufi-theologian al-Ghazzali (d. 1111) pictures Muhammad saying in the afterlife scene, 'I am the right one! I am the right one [to intercede] insofar as God allows it for whomever He wills and chooses.' God then says to him, 'O Muhammad, lift your head and speak, for you will be heard; seek intercession and it will be granted'.[19] Once again, the popular portrait of Muhammad finds him as an extremely important persona in the salvation of his community, someone far more significant than simply the recipient of the revelation of the Qur'an. Islam very much revolves around its twin sources of authority, the Qur'an and Muhammad, with both of those entities being firmly situated in the pre-history of the community in Arabia.

PART TWO

The emergence of Islamic identity

CHAPTER FOUR

Political action
and theory

Religion and the Arab expansion

Muslim sources, frequently confirmed by the unintentional witness of
contemporaneous Greek and Syriac writers, make it clear that the Arabs
came surging out of the Arabian peninsula in the seventh century, with
the initial attack on Damascus in 635 (the city being taken finally in
637), Ctesiphon in 637 and Jerusalem in 638. The area had been made
ready for such an invasion by the political situation of the Near East as
sketched in chapter 1 above. A critical matter of dispute among historians
is the extent to which religion was a motivating factor in these wars of
expansion. The simple explanation that religion, in the common sense of
the word, provided the underpinning of the whole phenomenon is not
necessarily supported by the archeological data available; nor is it
substantiated by the historical texts, at least when they are no longer
interpreted in the light of theological back-reading. What appears fairly
plain is that, in the first century of Arab rule in the Near East, a religious
ideology was being employed both by those in power and by those
struggling for power; it was by means of this ideology that authority was
established in the community. Once again then, one must be careful in
speaking of the religion in the earliest period: to call it 'Islam' easily leads
to the glossing over of the difference between what was conceived then
and what the religion had become by the beginning of the third Muslim

47

century, when a fixed religious system had certainly emerged (although its orthodox form was still at least a century off even at that point). Some scholars have suggested that we should refer to this early religion of the Arabs as 'Hagarism', a word derived from the name used in some Greek and Syriac sources when talking about the 'Muslims'.[1] Others have suggested a term such as 'Muhammadanism' or even 'Arab monotheism'.[2] Be that as it may, in general some of the most important evidence for making some distinction between the earlier and later roles and forms of the religion in the area comes from political actions of the early rulers of the conquered territory, especially as the rulers affected the religious ideology and symbolism through their employment of it.

History of the Arab conquests and empire

Abu Bakr took over rule of the community in the position of 'caliph' (*khalifa*), upon the death of Muhammad in the year 632; he was selected by a group of elders, according to traditional reports, as being the person most qualified to rule. At that time the Arabs controlled no territory outside Arabia, as far as the contemporary sources let us know. It was under Abu Bakr's leadership that early victories in Iraq in 633 (the city of Hira) took place. The year 634 saw the beginnings of the conquest of Syria as well as the accession of 'Umar ibn al-Khattab, the second caliph. Syria gradually fell into Arab hands with the battle of Yarmuk in 636 inflicting a crushing defeat on the Byzantine army. Damascus, Antioch, Jerusalem and finally the whole Syrian area came under Arab control by 638. Meanwhile, Iraq was falling also, with the conquest of Ctesiphon (Mada'in) and the defeat of the Sasanian army in 637, followed by the founding of the garrison towns of Basra and Kufa in 638. By 641, the Sasanian empire was coming close to its final end, with virtually all of Persia open to the Arabs after the battle of Nihavand. The conquest of Egypt was begun in 639 and completed by 642. With 'Umar's death in 644, 'Uthman ibn 'Affan, the third caliph, took over; in his time, the armies made westward gains, coming near the Roman outreach of Carthage by 647, but the area proved much harder to subdue than the former Sasanian or Byzantine territories. Some of the islands of the Mediterranean came under Arab domination at this time, with Cyprus being taken in 649 and Rhodes and Crete occupied shortly thereafter; these conquests came as a result of the emergence of Arab sea power, which provided a means of defence for the armies against the initially superior Byzantine naval forces.

'Uthman was assassinated in 656, reputedly by a group of disaffected tribesmen from Egypt, and his rule was followed by that of 'Ali ibn abi Talib, cousin and son-in-law of Muhammad. 'Ali's position was challenged, however, by a group consisting of 'A'isha (one of the widows of Muhammad), Talha, and al-Zubayr, members of the group of close followers of Muhammad. The 'Battle of the Camel' was the result of this uprising, leading to the death of Talha and al-Zubayr, and the removal from a position of influence of 'A'isha. 'Ali was effectively in charge until a kinsman of 'Uthman, Mu'awiya, revolted. Power and authority were clearly the issues at stake in this civil war once again, although rivalries between groups of Arabs, both on matters of tribal loyalties and political/practical problems, have also been seen to be partially responsible.

'Ali and Mu'awiya met in what is known as the 'Battle of Siffin' which was, in the end, submitted to arbitration because of the indecisive outcome of the clash. The fact of submitting the matter to this sort of resolution led to a clear erosion of 'Ali's power for it acted to legitimize the challenge to his position as ruler. Probably by the year 660, Mu'awiya had full control of his home province of Syria. In 661, 'Ali was murdered by a rebel, creating a situation in which Mu'awiya was able to take over Kufa in Iraq, the power base of 'Ali, and emerge as the clear leader; thus was formed what became the Umayyad dynasty which lasted until 750. Certainly not all the people rallied behind Mu'awiya; some supporters of 'Ali, who gained the name the Shi'a, or 'party', of 'Ali, remained outside the control of the new leader. Others who are thought to have felt that the whole process was somehow illegitimate, declared themselves opposed to both sides and became known as the Kharijites, those who had 'gone out' from the community. The stance of such people plays a major role in the discussions over theological issues, as will be discussed in the next chapter. It is tempting to see people such as the Kharijites as the earliest bearers of the religious impulse which became Islam; thus their rejection of the political powers of the day may be seen in religious as well as political terms. Such a reading of history remains at this time fairly speculative, however.[3]

Meanwhile, the expansionist wars were continuing. By 661, the armies had already arrived in Afghanistan, making their way to India, as far as the Indus river and the province of Sind. Under a succession of Umayyad rulers, the armies went into central Asia with Bukhara being raided in 674 and Samarkand in 676, although it took until 711 for the area to be fully settled. Sporadically from 670 on, Constantinople was besieged, although it was never actually captured until 1453 under the Ottomans. Eastern sections of Anatolia and Armenia fell towards the end of the seventh century. Likewise, the conquests in the west continued, with Kairouan in present-day Tunisia founded in 670, and Carthage finally falling into Arab hands in 693. From there, the armies went to the Atlantic and crossed into Spain in 710, taking over Toledo in 712. Southern France was invaded in 725 but the over-stretched army was stopped from further incursions into Europe by the Battle of Tours in 732.

Mu'awiya ruled from 661 until 680 when he died and, by previous arrangement, the leadership of the empire went to his son Yazid. This transfer of power did not go uncontested. Almost immediately upon assuming power, Yazid faced a rebellion by one of 'Ali's sons, Husayn, whose efforts appear to have been pitiful, although his actions have had an enormous mythological power in later Shi'ism. A more serious and lasting challenge came from 'Abd Allah ibn al-Zubayr who was a member of the Quraysh tribe to which Muhammad had belonged and a resident of Medina. Amassing power in his home base, Ibn al-Zubayr was attacked by Yazid's Medinan governor in 680 but he was able to flee to Mecca, where he gained power especially when Yazid died in 683. His rebellion continued, even reaching such an extent that he was the most significant leader within the Arab empire for a certain period of time, until a strong power re-emerged within the Umayyad family, that of 'Abd al-Malik (685–705) and he was defeated. It was also under the rule of 'Abd al-Malik and his son al-Walid (705–15) that the final surge of the conquests in the east and the west were accomplished.

By 744 the power of the Umayyads was being challenged again and despite a strong ruler, Marwan II (744–50), an apparently Shi'ite-inspired rebellion fomented in the eastern province of Khurasan. This eventually led to civil war and the rise of the 'Abbasid dynasty in 750. The Shi'ites were quickly disavowed by the new rulers but the change in ruling families did have far-reaching consequences beyond the actual political structure of the state. A socio-economic restructuring of the empire took place, with the partial removal of the 'old guard' who were entrenched in positions of power within the social system and the eventual emergence of a new and powerful class of bourgeois and religiously devoted scholars. The capital of the empire was moved from Syria to Baghdad and this action provided the impetus for the splintering of various areas of the new empire. For the western reaches of the empire, this eastward shift of the caliphal seat of power was cited as an example of the lack of interest exhibited by the central administration for the more far-flung portions of the empire. A descendant of the Umayyads, 'Abd al-Rahman, became the independent ruler of Spain in 756. Similar independence movements affected North Africa during the late eighth and ninth centuries. Likewise separate dynasties emerged in the East, especially in the provinces of Khurasan and Transoxiana, in the ninth century, leading eventually to the Buwayhid family taking over Baghdad itself in 945 and reducing the caliph to a person of little influence who acted only as a puppet of the real military rulers. The Mongol takeover in 1258 spelled the end even to this remnant of 'Abbasid caliphal prestige.

The role of Islam in the early Arab empire

Such were the political events of the early centuries and of the story of these conquests, there is little reason to harbour substantial doubts concerning their over all chronological ordering. What is significant, however, is that during this period the gradual emergence of the classical form of Islam may be seen. But just what was the role of Islam in all of this political activity? What was the role of politics in enunciating the classical form of Islam? What was the position of the caliph as the leader of the community and how did he use the idea of Islam in his ruling of the community?

The Dome of the Rock and its significance

During the rule of the Umayyad caliph 'Abd al-Malik an event of major significance took place; the Dome of the Rock in Jerusalem was built. This is the oldest extant building of Islamic architecture and one which can be dated with significant precision due to the presence of an important inscription which is found on both sides of the outer arched colonnade within the building. The inscription was tampered with by al-Ma'mun, the 'Abbasid caliph (ruled 813–33). He had ordered some repairs done to the Dome in about the year 831 and he appears to have followed a general policy of attempting to obliterate signs of the accomplishments of the earlier Umayyads. Significant original information still remains in the inscription, however, apparently due to an 'oversight' on the part of those who changed it. The end of the inscription, at the east end of the south face on the outer band of the colonnade reads: 'The servant of God 'Abd Allah the *imam* al-Ma'mun, commander of the believers, has built this Dome in the year 72 [=691], may God accept

THE DOME OF THE ROCK

N
↑

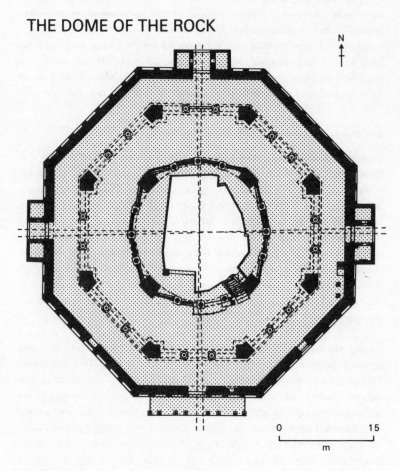

0   15
m

Source: E.T. Richmond, *The Dome of the Rock in Jerusalem*, Oxford, Oxford University Press, 1924, p.6

him'.[4] Not only is the shade of the mosaic in which the inscription has been written different when the name of the caliph is stated, but also the name is written in crowded characters. Most telling, however, is the fact that the date which is given (and is written in mosaics of the same shade as the rest of the inscription) is that of 'Abd al-Malik who, as all the other sources tell us, had the Dome built and ruled from 685 to 705. A similar tampering is also witnessed on the copper inscriptions over the north and east doors which are also held to have been written in the time of 'Abd al-Malik, according to the evidence of the shape of the script itself.

Why was the Dome of the Rock built?

Later Muslim historians provide several reasons for 'Abd al-Malik having built the Dome. As stated earlier, during the revolt of Ibn al-Zubayr, control of Mecca fell to the rebel leader. In order to assert his authority and independence, 'Abd al-Malik, according to this tradition, had the Dome of the Rock built as a place of pilgrimage. This explanation attempts to account for the unique (within Islam) architectural style of the Dome, for it is not a mosque nor is it an imitation of the Ka'ba. It is, however, clearly a place where pilgrimage type activities – especially circumambulation – were designed to take place within the colonnaded passageways. Modern historians have objected to this interpretation, suggesting that it is unlikely that any caliph would attempt to displace Mecca as a point of pilgrimage for this would be likely to entail, as a result, the total rejection of that person's legitimacy to be ruler of an 'Islamic' state. Such an objection, however, is based upon a supposition that the pilgrimage to Mecca was already a central symbol of nascent Islam. It would seem just as possible to conceive that, in the era of 'Abd al-Malik, the activity of pilgrimage was being used as a political symbol and that two pilgrimages, one in Mecca under Ibn al-Zubayr and another in Jerusalem under 'Abd al-Malik, emerged at roughly the same time in competition with one another.

Another suggestion classically put forth to explain the existence of the Dome of the Rock is that it was a sanctuary built to commemorate the 'ascension' (mi'raj) of Muhammad as related above in chapter 3; the rock from which Muhammad ascended into heaven is covered by the commemorative Dome. Such an interpretation is clearly late, however, for no part of the inscription of 'Abd al-Malik found in the building makes any reference to this journey; nor do any of the texts which are found in the colonnade inscription (texts which are also found in the Qur'an) even contain an allusion to this myth.

Finally, texts from various Muslim historians suggest that the Dome was built to rival the beauty of the Christian Holy Sepulchre in Jerusalem.[5] This is an account which has echoes throughout Islamic history, for example in the accounts of Sultan Ahmet I and his commissioning the architect Mehmet Aga early in the seventeenth century to build the Blue Mosque (Sultan Ahmet Camii) in Istanbul directly opposite the Christian church of Justinian, Haghia Sophia, dedicated in 537, in order to rival its magnificence.

The interpretation of the Dome of the Rock

This latter explanation may, in fact, contain an element which is meaningful historically when the building is interpreted as a whole in its architectural form and in light of the contents of the inscriptions. It would appear that the desire of the builder was not only to rival but to outshine all other buildings and, most importantly, to symbolize the triumph of the conquerors over the land and over the rival religions. The Dome of the Rock embodies the arrival of nascent Islam and underlines the religion's rising presence. It is a piece of work representing the ultimate propaganda of the Arab rulers over their subjects through the use of religion. That is why the building is so important to any understanding of the rise of Islam. Still, though, why the Dome should have been built over this specific rock in Jerusalem remains unclear; a suggestion that in fact the Muslims were completing a Christian project from an earlier time is possible but, once again, there does not seem to be an overwhelming amount of evidence for such a notion.[6]

The inscription in the Dome of the Rock

The evidence of the inscription on the colonnade (which people circumambulating the rock would see and read, especially the one on the inner surface) suggests significant aspects of the Arab propaganda effort. The outer face of the colonnade contains a series of passages, found today in the Qur'an, which comprise five groups of short phrases each emphasizing the unity and absolute unrivalled power of God, that He has had no offspring and that Muhammad is His messenger. The text on the inner face declares the unity of God and Muhammad's status and continues with verses addressed to the 'people of the book', admonishing that no mistakes be made in religion, declaring the Trinity to be false and telling of the correct view of Jesus, the spirit from God. 'Do not speak of three (gods)', one of the passages warns. The polemical aspect of the inner text especially is clear. The testimony to the development of Muslim doctrine is significant also; here we have evidence of the status of key beliefs in Islam – the non-messianic and non-divine status of Jesus, the acceptance of a multiplicity of prophets, Muhammad's receipt of revelation and the designation of the religion itself by the name of Islam.

The architectural style of the Dome of the Rock

The distinct architectural style of the building is also significant in understanding the rise of Islam. The Dome itself is clearly modelled after Syrian Christian churches – it may be seen as the final achievement of the Byzantine architectural style[7] – although it has also been suggested that it contains in its decorations many Sasanian traits; certainly the only true Arab element in the building is the inscriptional calligraphy. A close connection has been noted between the Dome and various earlier buildings of the Byzantines, including the Church of the Holy Sepulchre and the cathedral in Bosra (southern Syria) built in 512;[8] the resemblance extends most importantly to the geometrical structure of the buildings themselves. By employing a clear tradition in Byzantine architecture, the Dome was able to provide evidence to the conquered people of the power of the new rulers. It should be noted that circumambulation appears to have been practised by Christians who went around the tomb of Jesus in the rotunda of the Holy Sepulchre; thus, the entire rite connected to the building in early times is likely to have been one which would have reinforced this assertion of authority.

It has also been suggested that the inscription of 'Abd al-Malik inside the Dome aimed to provide spiritual guidance to the believers and to show the fundamental difference between Christianity and Islam. That is, the Dome was built as a symbol of, and a vehicle for, the emergence of the self-definition of Islam over and against Christianity. This was done through the means of a splendid building, undoubtedly built to surpass the beauty of Christian churches but yet done in the model of a Christian edifice. It was situated in Jerusalem as a political symbol of triumph – symbolized in the very fact of its being built. Its construction served to indicate the gradual emergence of Islamic identity in a form expressive and meaningful for all to behold.

Indeed, one of the statements in the inscription refers to Islam as 'the religion with God' (compare Qur'an 3/19); from this point on, therefore, those in power are clearly arguing for their religion 'Islam'. The copper inscription over the north door also refers to Muslims as those who believe in God, what He revealed to Muhammad, and that there is no difference among the prophets, all of whom God sent (compare Qur'an 2/135). Additionally, the inscription indicates the direction of early theological self-definition in the sense that the emphasis on Christianity can be seen to suggest Islam's supercession of the Christian faith especially in light of its doctrine of Jesus. The connection of the rock over which the Dome is built to King David and the Jewish Temple may well be intended to suggest both the fulfilment of the promise of Judaism, as well as the abrogation of that dispensation – Islam has taken over the Davidic heritage in both religious and political ways.

The Caliph and his authority

The Dome of the Rock represents, therefore, a conscious attempt on the part of 'Abd al-Malik to assert the authority of the new rule and to champion the new religion of Islam. That this was very much a personal matter, one which established his own authority not only among the new subjects of the empire but also among the members of the Arab community, appears to be evidenced by the self-conception of the caliph in this early period. Thus, while the Dome of the Rock provided the *symbol* of the caliph's authority, the actual conception of the position provided the *source* of his authority.

Classical Islam reveals the phenomenon of religious authority residing with a scholarly elite and ultimately, it would be claimed, with the entire community. Some evidence has been interpreted to suggest, however, that this situation was not always so. Early on, the caliph, referred to by the title *khalifat Allah*, the 'representative (or deputy) of God', appears to have combined religious and political power, only to have the religious dimension of the power removed in the third Muslim century (as reflected in the later theory of the caliphate) in recognition of the *de facto* change in the power structure by that time. This revamping of power appears to have occurred at the hands of the scholars after a struggle involving an explicit attempt by the caliph to impose a specific religious system of thought which upheld his position and asserted his authority, as opposed to the efforts and interests of scholars who stood for their own independent authority.

The Caliph as khalifat Allah

Evidence for this position of the early caliph comes from the use of the title *khalifat Allah* as testified most significantly on coins from the reign of 'Abd al-Malik, the builder of the Dome of the Rock. This title is used in place of the later *khalifat rasul Allah* ('deputy of the messenger of God'), which was employed by the 'Abbasids alongside the earlier formulation, a fact which has often (mis-)led historians to believe that the two titles were directly equivalent.

Some recent scholarship[9] has suggested that the early caliph saw himself in a mode very similar to the Shi'ite Imam. Obedience to the caliph was deemed to be necessary for salvation because the caliph's authority came straight from God. For the individual in the early period, therefore, the choice of to whom to give one's allegiance was a religious one, since salvation was connected to it; at least, that was the argument that those in power appear to have been suggesting.

Concomitant with his stress on divine authority, the caliph acted as judge, creating the sacred law and acting as the reference point for decisions on difficult items of law. The argument was made that his rulings were based on the Qur'an, the practice (*sunna*) – not that of a fixed practice of the past embodied in the person of Muhammad but the practice as found in the territory concerned – and his own (superhuman) insight.

The 'inquisition' and the emergence of the scholarly elite

The early ninth century institution of the *mihna*, or 'inquisition', unintentionally put an end to this type of conception. The final result of the attempt to assert caliphal control over religious dogma embodied in this 'inquisition' was the emergence of an independent scholarly group of people (symbolized in the figure of Ahmad ibn Hanbal) in whom religious authority, to the extent which that was conceived to exist, was vested. Under the 'Abbasid caliph al-Ma'mun (ruled 813–33), various attempts were made to assert the power of the caliph in the community in a variety of areas concerned with religion. Significantly, beginning in 829, al-Ma'mun declared that all government officials and religious leaders must believe in the doctrine of the 'created Qur'an'; in 833 an 'inquisition', *mihna*, was initiated, such that only those who agreed with the caliph's dogma would be allowed to hold official positions. Those who refused, including Ahmad ibn Hanbal, were removed from their positions and imprisoned. This practice continued in the following reigns of al-Mu'tasim (ruled 833–42) and al-Wathiq (ruled 842–7). Al-Mutawakkil (ruled 847–61) put an end to the enterprise in 849 but by then it was too late.

The significance of the actual doctrine which al-Ma'mun and his successors tried to enforce is not as important as the act of their trying to impose it. Until this point, the authority of the caliph to enunciate and represent Islam, while not totally unchallenged, appears to have been accepted. That is, for the Umayyad and early 'Abbasid rulers, Islam was to a significant extent an ideological tool in the hands of the ruling powers. Al-Ma'mun's actions in attempting to enforce a version of Islamic orthodoxy backfired and led to the increasing prominence of those who rejected the caliphal authority in favour of the authority of a scholarly elite; their authority was said to lie in their transmission and interpretation of the Qur'an and the *sunna* of Muhammad. It is at this point that classical Islam as we know it today began to come into existence, as is reflected in the literary sources, virtually all of which stem from a time after this period and reflect those scholarly concerns, perceptions and interpretations of Islam.[10]

The final implication of this change in power structure is that religion and politics in Islam became disentangled. This is reflected in the later theories of the caliphate which recognized the fact that the two spheres were in practice separate although mutually supportive. The caliphate was defined as a 'form of government which safeguards the ordinances of the Sharia [=Muslim law] and sees that they are put into practice'.[11] Beyond that, the relationship between the person of the caliph and the actual mechanism of rule in both military and religious spheres was left open, such that practical realities of the Islamic empire could be accommodated to the theory and thus legitimized.

CHAPTER FIVE

Theological exposition

Theological writing in Islam

The previous chapter examined the role of the caliph and the learned classes in defining what Islam was to stand for, both theologically and politically. That discussion focussed on the role of authority; both within and behind the debates which went on in the early centuries, however, lie the actual doctrines which were to emerge as the central elements of Islamic self-definition in theological terms.

Certainly, no other element in the understanding of the formation of Islam has consumed such a great deal of intellectual effort among modern scholars as has the development of theology. Ironically, the resulting picture is one of considerable confusion, perhaps a consequence, once again, of the superabundance of late source material, the variety of ways of interpreting the data provided and the absence of a substantial quantity of texts traceable to the early period itself. Some relatively early works do exist but the picture they combine to create remains disjointed.

Theological writing is the end result of an attempt at religious self-definition; it attempts to enunciate what is believed within a certain group of people in terms of certain tenets. Within the Near Eastern milieu, various elements emerged among the religions of Judaism, Christianity and Islam which defined what they held in common and where they differed. The process of defining where Islam was to differ from the other religions and where it was to agree was what the early theological tracts attempt to accomplish. The texts do not do this in an explicit way, that is, they do not set up inter-religious comparisons; rather the debate went on under topics which were, to a great extent, already predefined within the general religious milieu and were then enunciated from within each religious perspective.

The emergence of Islamic theological identity

The basic elements of Islamic theology find their expression within the Qur'an and the *sunna* and are elaborated to some extent in works such as the *Sira* of Ibn Ishaq. In these contexts, the statements are not theology, of course, but rather simple credal formulae which have been isolated as being summaries of what Islam stands for. It took several centuries of scholarly reflection to mould this raw material into the mature formulations of Islamic faith. Belief in the oneness of God, in angels, in all the prophets and their scriptures, in the final judgement day, and in God's decree for humanity are often seen to be the core elements of faith for all Muslims; such simple summations arose, however, only after extensive reflection and debate concerning some very basic theological issues in the formative centuries of Islam.

The definition of a Muslim

From the available sources, one prime question emerges which seems to have been of major concern and may well have provided the stimulus toward developed theological writing. This was the issue of determining who was and who was not a Muslim. The later Muslim sources, which provide us with additional data on the origins of this dispute, picture it as first arising within the context of the history of the early Muslim community, in common with the general trend in the sources to put the origins of Islam back as far as possible. Disputes over succession within the Arab ruling groups appear to have been read and understood by later generations of Muslims in theological terms as well as political ones. At stake was whether 'Ali, the fourth leader of the Arabs after Muhammad, had the responsibility for avenging the death of his assassinated predecessor 'Uthman; the clan of 'Uthman, led by Mu'awiya, championed the claims of its kinsman, suggesting that 'Ali had lost rightful claim to rule because of his failure to follow up on this obligation. Civil war erupted and Mu'awiya and the Umayyad dynasty eventually took over. From today's perspective, there seems to be little reason to dispute the basic historico-political events. Muslim theological sources, however, see far more in these events and view them as paradigms for the discussion of issues of religious self-definition; they use these earlier events for discussion of the theological disputes which were, in fact, taking place at least a century after the fact. From a historical perspective, it is worth noting that the use of military force in trying to decide the issues concerning 'Uthman and 'Ali indicates immediately that there certainly was a great deal at stake at this time, and the issue really was far more involved than the question concerning the death of 'Uthman. In the later reading of these historical events, the notions of piety and the 'rightful' (i.e. moral) assassination of an 'unjust' ruler become the operative elements.

What comes forth from the sources is a picture of a variety of groups, each going under a name which is often provided with a connection back to the times of 'Ali and 'Uthman, each taking its own position on what constitutes the definition of membership within the emergent Muslim community. The reasons for being concerned with this question were likely to have been of both a practical and legal nature, over and above being the result of polemical discourse with Jews and Christians in the Near Eastern milieu.

The Kharijites

The Kharijites held a strict, activist position: all those who fall short of the total adherence to the Islamic precepts are unbelievers. Any of those who might happen to slip are thus rendered targets for the Islamic *jihad* against all non-believers; membership in the community, at the very least, provided protection from such attacks. In origin the group may well have been involved in even more basic discussions over the sources of authority in the community. Their slogan is said to have been *la hukm illa li-Allah*, 'there is no judgement except that of God', which would suggest that they held that only God, through His expression in the Qur'an, has made binding laws for humanity. At least in part, therefore, the Kharijites may be pictured as the scripturalist party who rejected those who attempted to supplement the single source of authority in the community with a notion of the *sunna*. For the Kharijites, this *sunna* was not a part of the divine revelation and therefore had no particular status in the framework of Islamic law. It may well be, then, that they are to be identified as a pietistic group in the context of emergent Islam, facing off against the asserted power and authority of the caliph and his *sunna*.[1]

Later, however, a part of the Kharijite ammunition against other groups was sought in *hadith* reports (that is, the *sunna* of Muhammad), which they saw as equating certain actions, for example adultery, with taking one out of the category of 'believer'.[2]

The Murji'a

The Murji'a adopted a conservative position, preserving the status quo. They argued that those who appeared not to be following the outward precepts of Islam must still be accepted as Muslims; only God truly knows their religious state. A profession of faith along with an inward assent to Islam was all that was required to confirm community membership; faith (*iman*) is 'of the heart and of the tongue'. The position starts with the emblem of theological identity implied by the questions concerning 'Ali and 'Uthman; were these two men guilty of sin? were their assassinations justified? The Murji'a are pictured in the sources as holding that the decisions on these questions must be left to God. As a theological position, this stance holds that 'works' are not a part of faith; that is, as long as a person professes belief in Islam (through the single 'act' of confession of faith) then that person is a Muslim. The actual performance of the ritual acts of Islam is not a criterion for member-ship in the community. This position was supported in the view of the Murji'a by the notion that in the Qur'an God called those who had confessed their faith (and that alone) 'believers'. According to Abu Hanifa (d. 767), good works will be rewarded primarily in the here-after:

> Whoever obeys God in all the laws, according to us, is of the people of paradise. Whoever leaves both faith and works is an infidel, of the people of the fire. However, whoever believes but is guilty of some breach of the law is a believing sinner, and God will do as He wishes with that person: punish the person if He wills, or forgive the person if He wills.[3]

In the here and now, it was frequently argued that any increase in faith as manifested in pious works was really only an increase in conviction on the part of the individual. The whole doctrine thus had a practical result in terms of the ease of conversion to Islam, as may be seen especially in the case of the spread among the Turks in Central Asia in the eleventh century of the later Maturidite theological school which followed Abu Hanifa's legal teachings.[4]

Abu Hanifa is generally pictured as the major early enunciator of the Murji'a position; certainly his name has become associated with documents which are seen as Murji'ite in their detail. One such document is *al-Fiqh al-akbar*,[5] another the *risala* ('letter') to 'Uthman al-Batti.[6] These documents, and others from the same school of thought, seem to have the preservation of the unity of the Muslim community as their central concern, as is suggested by the tolerant nature of the Murji'ite definition of faith.

The Traditionalists

A group generally termed the Traditionalists (often calling themselves, as do other groups, *ahl al-sunna*, 'the people of the *sunna*'; the name 'traditionalist' refers to the use of *hadith* materials in preference to the independent powers of reason) is generally connected to the figure of Ibn Hanbal (d. 855) in the early period. Its stance represents yet another position on this question of faith, essentially arguing that there are degrees of 'being Muslim': works do count towards one's status in the community although one can still be a believer and commit sin – there are, therefore, what may be termed 'degrees of faith'. This position is enunciated in works ascribed to Ibn Hanbal and to Abu 'Ubayd (d. 838), and is also found embodied in the books of *hadith*; it becomes the position of the later Ash'arite theological school and thus of the majority form of Islam. Ibn Hanbal is said to have summarized his position as 'faith consists in verbal assent, deeds and intention and adherence to the *sunna*. Faith increases and decreases.'[7]

Abu 'Ubayd was a scholar with broad intellectual interests who 'contributed pioneer studies of major significance, and in all of them he displayed a degree of erudition and reached a level of achievement which won the acclaim of contemporary scholars'.[8] Theologically, he argued that faith is submission to God through intention, statement of belief and works combined. Such faith varies by degrees, starting with the basic confession of faith and then building from there; whoever makes the first step is entitled to be called a Muslim (and thus, in practical terms, the doctrine has the same consequences as that of the Murji'a) but perfection of faith is something to be reached through works. One can be termed a believer on the basis of the statement of faith but there are ranks among the believers in accordance with the extent to which such people conform to the requirements of the religious system of Islam. The Muslim who commits a grave sin, therefore, is still to be termed a believer but is not as good a believer as someone who has not committed a sin; such a person is not a believer in the full definition of that term.

The Qadariyya

A fourth position in the over all debate became associated with some people from within a group known as the Qadariyya (for example, al-Hasan al-Basri, d. 728); here, as with the Murji'a, a person who professes faith in Islam is considered a member of the community, but those who can be observed not following the requirements of Islam are to be considered neither believers nor unbelievers, but somewhere in between – they are hypocrites. The end result in practical terms is, once again, the same as with the Murji'a, but the claim is being made that it is in fact possible to have an opinion about the status of a believer's adherence to Islam. The position does not distinguish, however, between levels of faith as does that of the Traditionalists.

The problem of free will and predestination

The Qadariyya were centrally involved in another theological dispute, one which is generally understood to have provided them with their name. The Qadariyya are those who discussed the issue of *qadar*, the preordination of events in the world by God. This group held to the position of the free will of humanity and was opposed in this matter by those often said to be more closely aligned to the political powers of the day. That is, the Qadariyya were on the more revolutionary wing of the theological groupings, for their espousal of free will was frequently connected to those agitating for a new political order, opposed to the Umayyad caliphs and their appropriation of both political and theological authority under the guise of having been appointed by God (and thus destined to fulfil this function).[9] If individuals were accountable for their actions, then so were governments, according to the Qadarite argument. The Murji'a are frequently pictured as those most supportive of the ruling powers, for their doctrine of faith as a personal concern did not facilitate judgements being made on anyone as to their status in the faith (beyond the actual statement of faith), whether that person be a peasant or the ruler.

The *Risala* (often translated 'treatise' in this instance) of al-Hasan al-Basri is generally seen as one of the earliest documents concerned with the argument for free will, although both the ascription of an early date to the text and its status as one of the earliest texts have been questioned.[10]

Al-Hasan argues in the treatise for the position of the individual's free will on the basis of the Qur'an; any suggestion made in the Qur'an that predestination is to be supported (as his opponents suggested) is to be countered by an interpretation of the passage in light of other statements. Most obvious in this regard, statements such as Qur'an 13/27, *God {sends} anyone He wishes astray*[11] (implying that the individual's fate is in the hands of God alone and there is nothing that can be done about it) are to be interpreted in the light of other statements such as Qur'an 14/27, *God {sends} wrongdoers astray*, where, it is asserted, the people are *already* astray (they are already 'wrongdoers'), by the act of their own free will, before God confirms them in their 'fate'. This became the standard interpretative tool of all those who argued for the free will position in Islam. From a more positive angle, the argument also ran that God says in Qur'an 51/56, *I have only created sprites {jinn} and men so they may worship Me*, meaning that all people must be free to worship God, for God would not command them to do something and then prevent them from doing it.

The Mu'tazila and the role of reason

Out of this political protest party of the Qadariyya, there appears to have developed a group known as the Mu'tazila. Clearly, this party adopted the theological stance of the Qadariyya. Most importantly, though, the Mu'tazila are generally credited with the perfection of the art of theological speculation in Islam in the form of *kalam* – the dialectical style of discussion where objections are put forth and then the response, in the form 'If they say . . ., it is said to them. . . .' While this style of discussion originated neither with the Mu'tazila nor even within Islam itself,[12] it was through this means that this group argued their position, one which was based around the dual principle of the justice and unity of God; working from this principle, all the implications were systematically laid out on the basis of the use of reason in the argumentation. While the Qur'an had its place in the discussions, it was not so much a source, when used by the Mu'tazila, as a testimony to the veracity of the claims which they were making. The basic assumptions of the Greek philosophical system (as understood and transmitted through Christian scholars) was the fundamental element underlying the whole position; it was argued that reason, and not only traditional sources, could be used as a source of reliable knowledge for human beings. The Mu'tazila were the first to introduce the Greek mode of reasoning and argumentation into Islamic religious discussions, changing the face of Muslim theology for all time as a result. Greek philosophical learning remained a discipline in and by itself among Muslims, being developed by people such as al-Kindi (d. c. 870), al-Farabi (d. 950) and Ibn Sina (d. 1037). The subject (known in Arabic as *falsafa*) was one which aroused the ire of many traditionalists and remained, for the most part, a rival to theology as a discipline, except in the hands of the Mu'tazila who used its tools to their advantage.

The justice of God

The notion of the justice of God, something demanded of the divinity by Greek logic, led to extensive discussions concerning the nature of the divinity and His relationship to humanity. 'Justice' for the Mu'tazila was equated with 'good', such that it was not possible to conceive that God would be unjust or evil. The basic Muslim principle that God will reward the true believers after death and punish the unbelieving wrong-doers is then connected to this: God must be just in assessing this punishment or reward and therefore humanity must have a fair chance to perform on the side of good or evil. Any sense of predestination must be removed from the Qur'an, therefore, by reinterpretation. Al-Khayyat (d. c. 912), the earliest Mu'tazilite author from whom we have a complete text directly, speaks, for example, of the Qur'anic notion of God 'sealing hearts':

> [the idea of 'sealing'] is not that He prevents people from doing what He orders them to do – He is above that! – rather, it refers to the name, the judgement and the testimony [concerning an act]. Do you not notice that He said [in Qur'an 4/155] *because of . . . their disbelief*? Thus He sealed their hearts because of what was in them of disbelief. [13]

The power to act given by God to humanity carries with it the power to decide which action to undertake; individuals must therefore be fully responsible for their own fate. Evil deeds must originate in individual actions and have nothing to do with God, a problem which the doctrine of predestination seems to create. However, unjust acts do seem to occur in nature – death of young infants, death through natural disasters and so forth. This theological problem was faced in a variety of ways by members of the Mu'tazila; some said, for example, that while God could have created a perfect world where such things did not happen, He chose not to. All this is, for the Mu'tazila, a necessary consequence of the doctrine of the justice of God.

The created Qur'an

The Mu'tazila had their moment of political support under the 'Abbasid caliph al-Ma'mun (ruled 813–33) with the institution of the *mihna* serving as an inquest body investigating the credal stance of leading figures at the time, as discussed in the previous chapter. Here the figure of Ahmad ibn Hanbal looms large for his role in resisting the Mu'tazilite creed. One issue was crucial at this time. Starting with the notion that the Qur'an was the word of God, the resultant discussion was over whether scripture was, therefore, created 'in time' or uncreated and thus existent from eternity. The argument, it is worth noting, was not a new one within the Judeo-Christian world, as may be witnessed by ideas of the 'pre-existent Torah' and Jesus as the Logos who 'was with God at the beginning'.[14] The Mu'tazila championed the notion of the created Qur'an as a part of their understanding of the inherent free will of humanity, often pointing to Abu Lahab and his being condemned to hell in *sura* 111; the Qur'an must have been created at the time of its revelation, they argued, for otherwise the fate of Abu Lahab would have been established beforehand, thus removing his freedom to determine his own fate. This issue was also related to the reality of God's speech; some took God's speaking to mean that He spoke as humans speak, with the organs of speech, a point which was then rejected as impinging upon God's 'otherness'. For a Traditionalist such as Ibn Hanbal, the reality of God's actually speaking must be so, because such is stated in the Qur'an.[15] In the beginning, it was this element which seems to have been crucial in the development of the argument and only later did the argument turn to one of the emergence of the Qur'an 'in time', as was the issue in the *mihna*.

The unity of God

This debate relates to the other important element of Mu'tazilite thought, the concept of the unity of God, *tawhid*. Polemic with Christianity and Manichaeism appears to have been part of the reason for the emphasis within Mu'tazilite thought on this doctrine and the use of the Greek mode of reasoning by protagonists from these other two religions may well account for the introduction of rationalism into Islam as well, occurring initially within this polemical framework. Al-Khayyat's work paints the portrait of a real threat posed by the radical dualism of the

Manichaeans, although it is likely that the Christian trinity was a far more important topic of discussion. The position adopted by most of the Mu'tazila was that God can only be described in negatives. Any attempt to ascribe positive attributes to God was seen as impinging upon His unity, for such would suggest that He could be divided into a series of eternal aspects. The closest that one may come to saying something positive about God would perhaps be to say that God is 'knowing', but this 'knowing' occurs not by an attribute of God, but rather by and through God Himself in His essence. Once again, the parallels in these arguments to Christian discussions over the nature of Jesus in his relationship to the Father cannot be overlooked.[16]

De-anthropomorphization

One implication of this position on the unity of God was the emphasis on de-anthropomorphization of the divinity[17] especially as He is described in the Qur'an. Any suggestion that God might have a 'face' (Qur'an 2/272, 6/52 etc.) or be 'sitting upon a throne' (Qur'an 2/255 etc.) in reality was to be rejected and taken as a metaphorical statement; no reference to the human form could be applied to God in its usual meaning. God's 'face' was to be understood as His 'essence', according to al-Khayyat, for example. Thus, the discussion conducted during the *mihna* over the status of the Qur'an was not related only to the matter of free will. For the Mu'tazila at least, both major aspects of their doctrine, unity and justice, were encapsulated in the idea of a created Qur'an; an eternal Qur'an would suggest an attribute of God (speech) which existed separately (in the concept of the 'heavenly tablet') alongside God, impinging thereby on His unity, as well as suggesting predestination of events.

Revealed law and reason

The role of reason for the Mu'tazila was such that the main principles of the conduct of life – the principles of good and evil – were seen to be discoverable by any rational human. Revelation is necessary only in order to supplement what reason can discover, especially in such matters as the ritual law of Islam. For example, 'Abd al-Jabbar (d. 1025), one of the last major medieval Mu'tazilite thinkers, suggests that the eating of meat would not be allowed in Islam if it were not for the fact that scripture supports the practice; reason, therefore, cannot be seen to provide necessarily the full delineation of the law and scripture must provide the additional pointers needed.[18] Revelation also serves to motivate people with its emphasis on the promise and the threat of the afterlife; the Mu'tazila recognized that humanity was in need of guidance and that, in its 'natural state', it would not follow the dictates of reason.

The fall of the Mu'tazila

This view of the role of reason is significant in terms of the ultimate fate of the Mu'tazila, for it implied that the legal scholars of Islam had, in fact, no particular claim to sole possession of the right interpretation of all Muslim dogma. For the Mu'tazila, all humans are in theory capable of making the correct decision on issues of faith and law because of their God-given intellect. There is, therefore, implicit in this stance an anti-jurist bias that may well have proved to be part of the cause of their eventual downfall. Agitation by the scholarly elite whose job it was to provide the interpretation of the law is likely to have brought about the eventual political action, by the caliph al-Qadir in the years 1017 and 1041, of demanding a profession of faith which rejected the Mu'tazilite stance. This finally put a stop to the movement[19] (at least until more recent times when it re-emerged in the guise of modernism).

In the eleventh century, however, the Buwayhids, the rulers in Baghdad, were backing politically the remnants of the supporters of the fourth caliph, 'Ali, known as the Shi'a and the desire of the majority of the Muslims at the time (known as the Sunnis) to present a united front against this pressure was probably part of the reason for this final move against the Mu'tazila (whose theology had already influenced the Shi'ites by this time and was probably perceived as a threat by the Sunnis for that reason also[20]). So the eventual downfall of the Mu'tazila was undoubtedly a result of their doctrine as much as the political circumstances of the time.

Al-Ash'ari

Abu'l-Hasan al-Ash'ari (d. 935) emerged out of the context of the Mu'tazilite movement in the tenth century to enunciate a theological position midway between the scripturalism of the Traditionalists and the audacious rationalism of the Mu'tazilites, a position which was to last as the most significant statement of Islamic theology. In his book *al-Ibana* for example, he uses the *kalam* style of argumentation, setting up questions to be posed to his opponents who are stipulated to be especially the Mu'tazilites who 'interpret the Qur'an according to their opinions with an interpretation for which God has neither revealed authority nor shown proof.'[21] To the questions which he poses in his arguments, he responds: 'If they say "yes", then it follows that . . . or if they say "no", then it follows that . . .' with the arguments being pursued to the point of logical contradiction or contradiction with the twin sources of authority in Islam, the Qur'an and the *hadith*.

Al-Ash'ari's method was based upon extensive use of the Qur'an and the *hadith* in order to formulate his rational arguments. He fully supported the position of predestination, God being pictured in the Qur'an clearly as all-powerful and all-knowing; that God should not know and not be in control of what people were doing is clearly a problem if the free will position is embraced. For al-Ash'ari, God creates the power for people to act at the moment of action (God being the only one who actually has the power to create) yet the individual is responsible for all he or she does. This responsibility is referred to as 'acquisition', that is that people 'acquire' the ramifications of their actions, perhaps to be thought of as similar to the workings of the 'conscience' in modern terminology. Says al-Ash'ari, 'No human act can occur without His willing it, because that would imply that it occurred out of carelessness and neglect or out of weakness and inadequacy on His part to effect what He wills.'[22]

God's attributes are real for al-Ash'ari because the Qur'an clearly states them and so it must be meaningful to speak of God's hand and God's face; de-anthropomorphization was one of the central elements of Mu'tazilite thought which al-Ash'ari denounced, for he saw it as a symbol of rationalist excesses and willful ignorance of the sense of the Qur'anic text. Still, he did not wish to deny that reason indicates that speaking of these attributes of God would seem problematic when put in conjunction with an infinite God. His solution was to speak of the reality of the attributes but that these are not attributes in the same way that humans have such: God does have a hand, but we just 'do not know how' this is to be conceived. The phrase *bila kayf*, 'without knowing how', became a key term in Ash'arite theology, to be used whenever reason and the Qur'an or *hadith* met head-on in conflict.

Al-Ash'ari saw the Qur'an as the eternal and uncreated word of God, precisely because it was the word of God and, therefore, must partake in the character of His attributes. Those attributes (most importantly knowing, powerful, living, hearing, seeing, speech, and will)[23] are all strongly affirmed by al-Ash'ari who argued that if God does not have these attributes in reality, then He is somehow deficient and that, of course, cannot be the case. For example, al-Ash'ari states:

> one who is living, if he be not knowing, is qualified by some contrary of knowledge such as ignorance, doubt or other defects. . . . But if He had been ever qualified by some contrary of knowledge, it would have been impossible for Him ever to know. For if the contrary of knowledge had been eternal, it would have been impossible for it to cease to be; and if it had been impossible for it to cease to be, it would have been impossible for Him to have made works of wisdom. Hence, since God has made such works, and since they prove that He is knowing, it is true and certain that God has always been knowing, since it is clearly impossible for Him to have been ever qualified by some contrary of knowledge.[24]

Al-Maturidi

Abu Mansur al-Maturidi (d. 944) was another of the tenth century theologians whose influence at the time seems to have been significant in the emergence of Sunni Islam. Living in Transoxiana, he attacked the doctrines of the Mu'tazila and set down the foundations of his theological system. Like al-Ash'ari, al-Maturidi followed a middle path between Traditionalism and rationalism, forging an Islam which saw the written sources of the faith dominate but which found a place for the activities of the human mind.

Only a few texts have come down to us from al-Maturidi and his school but one of the most important, his *Kitab al-tawhid*, is available in Arabic.[25] The work commences by declaring that unconditional following of the teaching of another person is not valid: God has given humanity intelligence so that all may think and that gift must be used. This, of course, is a doctrine held in common with the Mu'tazila. Reason leads to knowledge, as do the senses and transmissions from the past, either from authoritative sources or from prophets. Reason must be used to judge the information provided by the other sources of knowledge. Reason also allowed knowledge of God before prophets were sent, a position contrary to al-Ash'ari who held that prophets were necessary and thus belief not incumbent upon those who had not been reached by God's messengers.

Following this in al-Maturidi's work come arguments concerning the temporality of the world, the necessary and eternal existence of God and that God is the creator of the world. This is all demonstrated in a rational way. Likewise, the oneness of God is proven and the matter of His attributes dealt with such that what the text of the Qur'an says about God must be believed, although we cannot know 'how' God is to be conceived of as 'sitting' on His throne, for example; this suggests a greater tendency towards interpretation of such matters than in al-Ash'ari. Al-Maturidi supports the idea of the free will of humanity, although God is, in fact, the only creator and He creates the actions of His creation; using the same notion as al-Ash'ari of individuals 'acquiring' their actions, al-Maturidi suggests that this acquisition is connected to the choice or intention which precedes an act. This is to be distinguished from al-Ash'ari's sense of acquisition being the contemporaneous coming into the possession of the capacity to act at the time of the action. Evil deeds, while predetermined by God, are the actions of the individual as a consequence of the choice and intention to do such acts.

Al-Maturidi was the inheritor and perpetuator of the position of the Murji'a on the question of faith. Only two states exist: having faith or not having faith; the essence of faith is in the belief in one's heart but there must be some practical consequence of this within Islam.

For a century after the death of al-Maturidi, his teaching does not seem to have been of much importance, not drawing the attention of even Ash'arite opponents for some 150 years. The reason for this neglect undoubtedly lies in the fact of al-Maturidi's residency in Samarqand and thus being well away from the centre of Islamic intellectual activity; his doctrines appear to have remained of local concern to the community in that region, with little external note taken of the development. The position of al-Maturidi is generally presented as being a development of Abu Hanifa's stance which had already spread to Samarqand by al-Maturidi's time. Abu Hanifa's position as eponym of the Hanifite legal school allowed al-Maturidi's later followers to argue for the acceptance of their theological stance in areas outside Samarqand which were already dominated by the Hanifite legal school; they argued this on the basis of this previous relationship between the two schools of thought.

The spread and the eventual success of the school was a result of the conversion of Turks in Central Asia to Islam of this Hanafite–Maturidite persuasion. The liberal theological implications of Hanafite juridical requirements – such that faith is present in the individual even if all religious duties are ignored – is thought to have allowed for the gradual conversion of these nomadic peoples. With the expansion of the Turks, starting in the Seljuk period, Maturidism came to the attention of other groups in the Islamic community. The theological position of later Maturidism is represented for example in the *'aqida* or creed of al-Nasafi (d. 1142) which has proved popular throughout the Muslim world, attracting many commentaries and elaborations even from Ash'arites.[26] In form, the creed presents what had become the classical sequence of argumentation, starting with the enumeration of the sources of knowledge and moving through discussion of God and His attributes and His nature, belief and the communication from God via messengers to be concluded by a discussion of life in the world. The whole theological position is thereby argued to be one cohesive whole, leading its reader from simple observations on how we know things to the compelling implication that therefore the Muslim way of life is the true and divinely desired one.

The role of theological writing

Theological writing became an art in Islam, although, as will become clear in the next chapter, it never had the place of honour in the community which legal discussions held. To some extent certainly, this is because the theological enterprise was dedicated more to the theoretical than the practical aspects of Muslim life. Islam is, to a great extent, predicated upon the idea of responding to the call from God through action; thus, the most crucial and relevant discipline to the vast majority of Muslims has been the one which guides human behaviour – Islamic law – rather than theology with its dedication to the realm of human thought. Theology did provide some of the intellectual basis for the enunciation of the distinction between Islam on the one side, and Judiasm, Christianity, and a multitude of other 'lesser' religions on the other; it was, therefore, a crucial element in the formation of Islam as an independent and individual mode of existence within which a religious way of life could be led.

CHAPTER SIX

Legal developments

The sense of 'law' in Islam

Sunni Islam (as compared to Shi'i, to be dealt with in chapter 8) is defined not by theological allegiance but by practice: following one of the four schools of law authenticated by the agreement of the community as being true implementation of the *sunna* or practice of Muhammad makes one a member of Sunni Islam. It is the individual believer's perspective on the law which becomes the central element of self-definition as a Muslim and which has thus evolved as the controlling element of the community's identification as a whole. Law in this sense, however, is a far broader concept than that generally perceived in the English word. Included in it are not only the details of conduct in the narrow legal sense, but also minute matters of behaviour, what might even be termed 'manners', as well as issues related to worship and ritual; furthermore, the entire body of law is traditionally viewed as the 'revealed will of God', subject neither to history nor to change.

The role of law in defining Islamic allegiance is emphasized by the fact that the theological schools of Islam, discussed in the previous chapter, gained their fullest support in the guise of appendages to groups of legal scholars; this support occurred in correlation to the attitudes manifested by those theological groups towards the roles of speculative reason and tradition in human life.[1] Theology, therefore, is not only subordinate in importance to law as a discipline but also incorporated within the whole legal framework.

The idea of sunna

The focal point of the law in Sunni Islam is the *sunna*, the concept of the practice of Muhammad, as embodied in the *hadith* and transmitted faithfully by Muhammad's followers through the succeeding generations down to the present. The *sunna* presents, for the individual Muslim, the picture of the perfect way of life, in imitation of the precedent of Muhammad who was the perfect embodiment of the will of God. The *hadith* reports are the raw material of the *sunna*, and must be sifted through by jurists in order to enunciate the details of rightful practice; the *shari'a* is the 'way of life' for the Muslim which has been developed by the Muslim jurists on the basis of certain jurisprudential principles, the *usul al-fiqh*.[2]

The history of Islamic law indicates that the *sunna* was not always perceived in this fashion, nor indeed was the *sunna* always considered to be the authoritative body of law for members of the community. Such a position took time and much argument before it emerged. It is to Muhammad ibn Idris al-Shafi'i (d. 820) that most of the credit must go in developing this aspect of the over all legal theory of Islam.

Before that transformation took place, however, it must be remembered that the concept of the law of Islam was a part of the emerging ideology and symbol system which provided a sense of identity to the Muslim community. Much of Islamic law, in substantive terms, can now be seen to reflect a Jewish background and concerns common to Judaism. At the same time, portions of the law appear to have developed in a pragmatic way, with the adoption of laws and practices as they were found in the lands which were conquered; this is especially evident in elements of Roman law which were adopted in the Muslim environment.[3] These two trends – Jewish and Roman – often merged, and they were reshaped as the distinct Muslim law emerged; this process was aided by many of the legal elements being recast by Muslims such that they were seen as emerging from the context of the *jahiliyya*, as was suggested above in chapter 1.

In the early community, law was employed as a tool by which unity was imposed from above and for which an authority was needed to justify the requirements of that law. In the earliest period after the conquests, it would appear that the caliphs themselves were pictured as the authorities within the community on legal matters[4] and it took some time before a unifying concept of the authority of Muhammad as enunciated in the notion of the prophetic *sunna* actually emerged.

When the word *sunna* is used in texts from the early period it refers not to the *sunna* of Muhammad but to the *sunna* of the caliphs and/or the *sunna* of a particular area, often combined with a sense of an ideal behaviour which is normative.[5] That is, as the Arab territories expanded and Islam became the emblem of that region, the law developed in a non-uniform manner under the general umbrella of 'Islam'. Each local area developed, in a pragmatic style, a law based upon the practice of its own region. This appears to have been supplemented to some degree by the centralized efforts of the caliph to unify his domain.

The emergence of schools of law

From the early stages of developing the law in a pragmatic and authoritative way, various 'schools', *madhhab* in the singular, emerged, in which people sharing common positions derived from their own personal legal deductions gathered together. The schools formed around the name of a single person, a teacher who had instructed students in the law, although it is doubtful that any of the individuals actually intended to start a 'school' as such.[6] The schools themselves did not (and do not now) demand adherence or conformity, nor did the term *madhhab* imply any particular teaching activity. What a school shared was a common interest in a specific body of legal material which, in one way or another, was connected to the eponymous founder of the school and his followers.

There can be little doubt that these schools emerged through the pious motivation and efforts of those involved in the study of law, combined with the emergence of a class of scholarly elite whose desire it was to wrest authority from the hands of the caliph. For Muslims to be sure that they were fulfilling the will of God as completely as possible, it was necessary that every detail of the law be expounded; this required that every aspect be discovered. As new situations arose, never before encountered within Muslim society, it was the jurists' responsibility to discover 'the will of God' in such instances. The rules of jurisprudential theory (*usul al-fiqh*) were eventually established in order to allow individual jurists to make these sorts of decisions in an orderly and 'Muslim' way.

The schools of law first emerged as local centres, reflecting the geographical diversity in the law from the beginning. Basra, Kufa, Medina, and Damascus are to be distinguished as the major regions developing their own traditions and influencing others. In Basra, the only lasting school of importance was that which became the Ibadi *madhhab*, a surviving relation of the Kharijite theological school; in Kufa there emerged the Hanafites, under the eponym of Abu Hanifa (d. 767) but developed by Abu Yusuf (d. 798) and al-Shaybani (d. 805), as well as various Shi'ite groups, including the Imamis, the Zaydis and the Isma'ilis. Al-Awza'i (d. 774) was associated with a school in Syria although it did not last very long. Medina produced Malik ibn Anas (d. 795) and provided the impetus, at the very least, for al-Shafi'i (d. 822). A later group, known as the Hanbalis, developed from Ibn Hanbal (d. 855) with a substantial debt to Medinan practices.[7]

The differences between these groups should not be exaggerated; the main contrast between the groups tends to be schematized best as a difference between the early groups in Iraq (who seem to have close contact with Jewish law) and those in Medina (who have a more 'liberal' attitude than their Iraqi counterparts), with the later schools following the Medinan position.[8] The issues at stake were generally matters dealing with customary practice and local conditions rather than disputes primarily over principles or methods. This sort of differentiation between the schools actually increased over time, as the schools developed what had been the early core of the law according to their own practices. Each school developed its own practice, its own *sunna*, which as time went on and authority was sought for individual practices, was traced back, first to prominent jurists in the past, then to companions of Muhammad and finally to Muhammad himself. This 'backwards growth' in authority is a tendency which has already been mentioned in chapter 3 in terms of the growth of *isnad*s: this is the same phenomenon but on a larger, more theoretical scale. The final result was the emergence of the *sunna* of Muhammad. The ultimate motivation behind this development was to create a structure of law which was Islamic through and through, by denying all foreign elements and justifying all the law in terms of the twin sources of Muslim life, the Qur'an and the *sunna*.

The role of al-Shafi'i

It took al-Shafi'i to make the *sunna* of Muhammad the authoritative source of law for all Muslims. Stimulating his efforts were claims made by Traditionalists to the effect that it was not sufficient for a jurist to simply assert that such and such an item was the *sunna* of Muhammad; there was, for these people, a need to prove each and every one of these statements.

This is where the role of the *hadith* with its *isnad* came in. The tendency to demand proof did not arise without a great deal of opposition, as evidenced most obviously within the Mu'tazilite movement which championed the use of reason in all matters of religion. For the most part, the schools of law as they had emerged by this point only accepted the arguments and the demands of the Traditionalists in so far as the latter's points would support the former's legal traditions. Where traditions from Muhammad could be seen to agree with a legal practice, all fine and good; there was not, at this point, any sense of changing the law in order to agree with the *hadith*.

Al-Shafi'i systematized what appears to have been chaos by developing a procedure for legal reasoning. While other scholars prior to him and contemporary with him, people such as Abu Hanifa, Abu Yusuf and al-Shaybani, were involved in this process also, modern scholarly research (especially that of Joseph Schacht) has shown al-Shafi'i to be the pivotal person in the emergence of the legal system of Islam as we know it. Al-Shafi'i demanded the use of systematic reasoning without arbitrary or personal deduction in formulating the law and thus he created a system that was far more cohesive on a theoretical level than had previously been the case. He argued for the authoritative *sunna* being that of Muhammad, a *sunna* which was to be found only in traditions transmitted from Muhammad himself; the acceptance of traditions from the companions was not to be considered sufficient. As al-Shafi'i states, 'the enactments of the Prophet are accepted as coming from Allah in the same way as the explicit orders of the [Qur'an], because Allah has made obedience to the Prophet obligatory'.[9] Furthermore, the Qur'an could not contradict the *sunna*; the *sunna* could only explain the Qur'an – such had to be the hierarchy of the sources of the law. A controlled notion of *naskh*, 'abrogation', was implemented in order to handle cases of apparent contradiction between and within the sources. The community of Muslims could be said never to be in contradiction of the *sunna* if they agreed on a certain practice: 'We accept the decision of the public because we follow their authority, knowing that, wherever there are *sunna*s of the Prophet, their whole body cannot be ignorant of them, although it is possible that some are, and knowing that their whole body cannot agree on something contrary to the *sunna* of the Prophet and on an error, I trust'.[10] This, in fact, must be the case in order to guarantee the transmission of *hadith* reports from Muhammad. It is not surprising, then, to note that the books of *hadith* were all compiled after the time of al-Shafi'i when the need for these sources was crucial.

The development of the schools of law

The major schools of law which have survived down until today had their major development in this period. The process was not one of transforming the local practice into a school as such, but of championing the doctrine of a teacher and the tradition which that teaching represented. In Kufa the Hanafite school including the star pupils al-Shaybani (who attributed his writings to Abu Hanifa and thus created the literary tradition which is the school of law, per se) and Abu Yusuf, became paramount and drew into their system the city of Basra; similarly, in Medina and followed by Egypt and Mecca, Malik ibn Anas, the author of *al-Muwatta'*, one of the first written compendiums of legal traditions, became central as the Maliki school, destined to find its major development in North Africa. Malik's book was an attempt to provide what traditions there were concerning a given topic and then to interpret them in light of the prevailing legal system of Medina. This latter element is the controlling factor in the whole book, rather than the traditions themselves.[11]

Al-Shafi'i's school was more personally based. He considered himself a member of the school of Medina but he ended up not following the tradition of that area; his efforts were directed towards combining the pragmatic approach and position of Medina with the demands of the Traditionalists for adherence to the *sunna* of Muhammad. Cairo proved to be the focal point of the development of his school, an area where al-Shafi'i spent the last portion of his life. The school emerged by the ninth century as one of the three major groupings which continued their efforts in developing the *shari'a*, or law, of Islam and out of which eventually came the *usul al-fiqh*, the principles of jurisprudence.

Principles of jurisprudence

The emergence of a fully enunciated theory of jurisprudence was not an instantaneous development of the law schools. The works of the earliest representatives of the law schools display a measure of disorder in their treatments of the law and rarely put forth the full basis of the reasoning in individual cases. It was not until the eleventh century that matters became more precise, so that definition of terms and reformulation of earlier decisions took place in works such as that of al-Sarakhsi (d. 1096) in the Hanafi school. This was not a simple reiteration of, or commentary upon, the earlier works but a creative reworking of the entire structure of the *fiqh* process.

According to the developed jurisprudential theory in Sunni Islam, there are four sources from which law can be derived: the Qur'an, the *sunna* of Muhammad, consensus (*ijma'*) of the community and/or the scholars, and analogy (*qiyas*). The first two provide the material basis upon which *qiyas* must operate. The vast majority of laws have, in fact, been fashioned by *qiyas* because the Qur'an and the *sunna* provide a fairly limited selection of detailed legal provisions.

An individual jurist first had to scour the works of previous jurists to find a precedent for a case under consideration or a case with similar facts. Should he not find one, he was faced with an unprecedented instance for which he would then employ *qiyas*, using as his starting point legal information found in the Qur'an, *sunna* or rendered absolute law by *ijma'*.

Qiyas works on the basis of finding the *'illa*, the common basis between a documented case and a new situation; this process depends upon the powers of deduction of the jurist and the results of his work will depend upon *ijma'*, the consensus of opinion, in whether or not it supports his judgement. Should the decision find general support, it becomes an irrevocable law and thus becomes the basis for further deductions by means of *qiyas*.

The role of consensus

The operation of *ijma'*, consensus, was a major issue in the development of the principles of jurisprudence, one which jurists took pains to prove was in fact a legitimate process substantiated by the Qur'an and the *sunna*; only in this way, it was argued, was it possible to distinguish between jurists who delegated to themselves the right to make laws (perhaps an accusation resulting from polemical discussions with Jews and Christians) and those who worked legitimately within the Muslim framework.

Ijma' functions to confirm rulings. While in theory this could take place at the time of a given ruling, in practice it occurred in retrospect. If no dissenting voices were heard by the time of the following generation, then it could be taken that *ijma'* had confirmed a ruling. *Ijma'* is often seen to be the most crucial element of the whole legal structure, for it is through its action that all elements are confirmed, especially individual *hadith* reports, but even, one might say, the Qur'an itself, which is only authoritative because all Muslims agree that it is so; this is emphasized by the fact that there is no centralized authority (in Sunni Islam) by which such a matter can be established. Muslim theorists, however, did not view the process in this manner, since they still needed to confirm the validity of *ijma'* as a concept by means of *hadith* and Qur'an. For them, the twin scriptural sources were authenticated by customary usage and their miraculous nature, rather than by consensus itself; thus no circular reasoning was involved.[12]

Reactions to the development of jurisprudence

The Traditionalist school which had demanded a complete rejection of personal reasoning was not totally satisfied by al-Shafi'i's compromise in working out the relationship between the sources of law. Ibn Hanbal who was the founder of the Hanbalite school, structured his thought on the principle of adherence to *hadith* in preference to personal reasoning. He manifested this attitude in his compendium of traditions, the *Musnad*. The anecdote is related that Ibn Hanbal never ate a watermelon because he could not find a tradition which suggested that Muhammad had done so or that he had approved of such.[13] Over the centuries, however, even this school, by the time it was accepted within the strictures of Islamic orthodoxy (or, more accurately, orthopraxy), came to the position of accepting the *usul al-fiqh* as enunciated by the other schools and thus embracing reasoning and consensus; watermelons were deemed acceptable.[14]

Another school emerged in the ninth century, known as the Zahiri group, founded by Dawud ibn Khalaf (d. 884). Claiming allegiance to the *zahir* or 'literal' sense of both the Qur'an and prophetic *hadith*, they rejected all aspects of systematic reasoning employed in the application of *qiyas*. This led to peculiar combinations of stances on the part of the school, appearing liberal in some instances – because it followed the letter of the law and did not extend it into the many other areas deemed analogous by other schools – and being far more strict in others. Ibn Hazm (d. 1065) remains the intellectual high point of this school which, in fact, lost much of its influence after his time.

The relations between the schools of law

By the end of the tenth century, the four schools – Hanafi, Maliki, Shafi'i, and Hanbali – had solidified their position to the extent that no further schools of law emerged from that point on. This did not mean that no further legal judgements were to be made but rather that the principles for which the schools stood and the legal stances which they had developed were to be the points within which all further discussion was to be conducted.[15]

The extent to which the schools disagree on points of law is of little concern to Muslims, for there is a tradition ascribed to Muhammad which addresses itself precisely to the situation: 'Difference of opinion in the community is a token of divine mercy'.[16] An attitude of mutual recognition among the schools has prevailed, such that orthodoxy in matters of law is defined only by acceptance of the roots of the law; this means that the Zahiri school was excluded due to its rejection of *qiyas*. Where a difference of opinion exists between the schools, it is to be taken that each opinion is an equally probable expression of God's will. On a matter seemingly as basic as the food laws, differences may be noted in whether certain animals are declared to be permissable or disapproved. The Hanifite school, for example, allows aquatic animals to be eaten only if they have the form of a fish. The Malikite school, on the other hand, consider all aquatic animals permissable. Both positions are considered equally valid and equally 'orthodox' for all Muslims.[17]

Law and morality

After considering a given legal case, a jurist is able to declare whether the resultant action itself is to be classified as being obligatory (*wajib*), recommended (*mandub*), permissible (*mubah*), disapproved (*makruh*), or forbidden (*haram*). Speaking in very broad terms, performance of obligatory actions will bring reward in the hereafter for the person concerned, while omission of the actions will bring punishment; recommended actions bring reward but no punishment for their omission. Forbidden actions will bring punishment for being committed but reward for being avoided, while disapproved actions bring reward for being avoided but no punishment should they be performed. The vast majority of actions fall into the 'permissable' category, the ramifications of which will not be felt in the hereafter. There are many subtleties in the application of these categories, but, in principle, they apply whether the concern is ritual, moral or legal; all activities are considered in the same way and all are under the rule of Islam. It is in the nature of this law, however, that even an act which is declared to be disapproved can still bring about a binding result. A marriage, for example, which has been dissolved in a way declared to be 'disapproved' is still considered to have been terminated in fact.[18] There is, thus, a separation between what might be considered law and morality, although it is all a part of one whole in the Muslim system, for all law ultimately has as its purpose gaining entry for the individual into paradise in the hereafter. At the same time, it is a sign of the realistic nature of Islamic law that the five moral categories of actions were adopted rather than a bipolar system of good versus bad (a position championed by the Mu'tazila at one point in history); the law recognizes that not all Muslims are going to be saints in every aspect of their behaviour and that they will need the urging forth towards perfection that the law can provide.

The role of the judge

The administration of the law in the Muslim community developed institutionally first under the Umayyads but came into its more lasting form under the 'Abbasids. A judge, known as a *qadi*, was appointed by the government to administer the *shari'a*. A central chief judge was also appointed by the government, to whom all other judges as well as the ruler himself would refer on all legal issues. He became the person who recommended the appointment of all the judges to the caliph and became the major legal counsellor of the ruler. The fact that all the judges (including the chief judge) were appointed by the government often led to conflicts; although in theory once a judge was appointed he was to be independent of the government, in practice such things as implementing decisions against high government officials was extremely difficult.

One of the qualifications for being a judge was, obviously, full knowledge of the Islamic law; other requirements included having sound sight and hearing, and being free (that is, not a slave), honest and a Muslim.[19] Such scholars were often the most strenuous upholders of Islam and they frequently saw the activities of the government as not being as fully 'Islamic' as desirable. Their ability to criticize those who gave them their jobs, however, was tenuous. This led to a great deal of discussion over legitimacy of rule and explains why there was such a lot of debate in Islam[20] concerning the need to follow an unjust ruler and the right of rebellion. The position of the judge and the legitimacy of the appointment to that post were never held to be affected by the nature of the ruling powers who appointed him (or her, for a woman, according to some lines of thought, could be a judge although she certainly did not have the right to rule in the imposition of the *hadd* penalties – those penalties specifically prescribed in the Qur'an for crimes such as adultery, stealing, armed robbery, drinking wine, false accusation of unchastity and apostasy). However, many of the leading jurists found it impossible to accept a position as *qadi* and made much of their refusal to do so; their principles always dictated that since, in their opinion, the ruler of the time was not fulfilling his responsibility to Islam, accepting a judicial appointment from such a person would be morally reprehensible.

The administration of justice

The judges depended upon the power of the government to put their decisions into action. This was crucial in issues of criminal justice for example. Although the law had been structured by the jurists such that essentially there were no crimes against the state – a crime is against another person or against God – the imposition of the prescribed penalties, especially the *hadd* penalties from the Qur'an, had to be enforced by some means. Eventually a police force was devised to handle such cases. Judges were further hampered by the terms of Islamic law which only allowed them to receive evidence that was submitted to them rather than being able to search it out or conduct interrogations; the law was founded on the notion that blameless witnesses would always tell the truth and that oaths of innocence would always be forthcoming from all honest persons. The jurists saw themselves 'in the role of spiritual advisors to the conscience of Islam rather than authoritarian directors of its practical affairs'.[21] The result of this was the inevitable situation of the political powers having to assume some of the responsibilities for direct administration of justice; several additional institutions emerged to deal with a variety of situations as a consequence.

Among the legal officials in the community was the 'investigator of complaints' (*nazar fi'l-mazalim*). This was an office originally designed to hear charges concerning the miscarriage of justice, and was thus to act as a check on judges; additional issues such as matters dealing with unjust taxes and enforcing the decisions of the *qadi*s were also in its purview. Later, the office emerged as a parallel system of justice, especially in matters of lawsuits; this was the result of the *mazalim* courts having powers which the *qadi*s did not enjoy: the right to double-check and investigate evidence, to restrain acts of violence and to refer people to binding arbitration.

An 'inspector of the market' (*muhtasib*, holding the office of the *hisba*) was also appointed, who was responsible for encouraging Islamic morality in general and thus provided the possibility of prosecutions in the general public interest. Specific duties of this office included matters relating to defective weights in the marketplace and commercial transactions where fraud or unpaid debts were suspected. Once again, the role of the judge was to a certain extent duplicated.[22]

The nature of Islamic law

Over all, Muslim law is recognized to be an 'ideal' system, one which will be corrupted and will suffer at the hand of corruption in the world. This is even more so because the law is, in the first instance at least, a theoretical development and enunciation by the jurists rather than a body of law emerging from precedents, although this position is tempered to some extent by practical considerations; the theoretical nature of the law may be best described, perhaps, as existing in tension with its practical aspects. To a degree, Islamic law is of a purely religious character, carrying with it only the threat of punishment by God; failure to follow the law of Islam concerning the prayer, for example, will not involve any juridical penalty in this world. An exception would be the case of a person who went so far as to deny the obligatory character of the prayer, which would then be evidence of the rejection of Islam itself. The law is flexible also to the extent that any law may be broken under duress or necessity; in such conditions, a given act previously considered forbidden becomes valid, including such things as eating pork when no other food is available or drinking wine in the absence of all other liquids.

One final implication of the character of Islamic law is to be noted in the treatment of Jewish and Christian communities living within territories controlled by Muslims. These groups were not subject to the specific provisions of Islamic law, precisely because it was for those who were Muslims alone. Rather, these communities were allowed to be self-governing, following their own legal codes and principles, although they were considered citizens at a lower level than their fellow Muslims with certain restrictions on their public rights and a requirement of paying of a special poll tax. Security of life, property and religion was guaranteed by the payment of this tax, but no new religious buildings were to be erected nor was the public display of religion to be allowed.[23] In practice, the tolerance shown for these communities fluctuated in the Muslim world according to the political and social pressures of the time but the theory, at the very least, echoed the character of Islamic law and its integrative religious nature.

CHAPTER SEVEN

Ritual practice

The notion of the 'five pillars'

To a person standing on the outside observing the presence of a religion, ritual is the most obvious sign of the character and existence of believers in that faith. Ritual activities and their attendant buildings, clothes and assorted paraphernalia provide the emblems of a religion and become, for the members of the religion themselves, modes for the expressions of their identity. Such ritual symbols also fulfil an obvious political function for the ruler, as a way of declaring his own dedication to the values embodied in the symbols and as a way of unifying his people behind him in one common symbolic expression.

For classical Islam, the notion of the 'five pillars' represents the epitome of the revealed law as enacted through ritual activity. The five actions – the witness to faith (*shahada*), prayer (*salat*), charity (*zakat*), fasting (*sawm*), and pilgrimage (*hajj*) – are duties for which each individual is responsible, separate from general ethics and rules for interpersonal relationships. They are an integral part of the belief system of Islam, being a part of the explication of theological statements of belief from at least the tenth century onwards.[1] The concept that 'five pillars' were the ritual centre of Islam emerged almost certainly within the second Muslim century; both the *hadith* collections of al-Bukhari (d. 870) and Muslim ibn al-Hajjaj (d. 875) contain early on in their books a report which states that Muhammad said, 'Islam is based upon five (principles)', followed by an enumeration of the five. While the term 'pillar' is not used in these reports (that term would appear to be a tenth century coinage), the isolation of these specific ritual activities is clear. Even earlier than the *hadith* collections, al-Shafiʻi (d. 822), in his *Risala*,[2] isolated prayer, charity, fasting and pilgrimage as among the central elements of the faith; it would appear that for him these elements had not become the actual defining factor of Islam, but the recognition of their prominence is present. A similar observation may be made for the *Muwatta'* of Malik ibn Anas (d. 795) whose work is organized such as to give prominence to the four rituals, but that presentation may well be the work of later editors, reflecting more developed strain of thought than that of Malik himself.

It is equally clear that none of the individual portions of the 'five pillars' was simply imposed upon new believers in Islam from the very beginning. Each ritual has its own history and its own significance, both elements often being very difficult to reconstruct. None of the rituals has its requirements fully expressed in the Qur'an.

The evidence of archeological remains from the earliest stages of the Arab conquests, for example in the area of the Negev desert, does not provide us with any clear indication of cultic or ritual emblems in this period either. Inscriptions found in these places reveal the rise of a religious ideology by their use of various religious invocations and also exhibit the emergence of places of worship. No clues are left, however, as to the character of this worship other than the observation that it took place alongside various pagan and Christian (and probably Jewish) worship practices.[3]

Testifying Muslim faith

The witness to faith (*shahada*) consists of repeating the two phrases 'There is no god but God', *la ilah illa Allah*, and 'Muhammad is the messenger of God', *Muhammad rasul Allah*. These phrases are recited in order to witness conversion to Islam. Such utterances have practical implications for the political order, therefore, entitling one to the privileges of membership in the Muslim community. The phrases must be recited in Arabic and prefaced by an honest statement of intention. The theologian al-Baghdadi (d. 1037) states that the person who utters the *shahada* must know 'the truth of the statement' and must repeat it 'out of understanding and with heartfelt sincerity'.[4] The *shahada* is repeated as a part of the Muslim prayer, *salat*, and thus gains more of a sense of being an oft-repeated ritual than simply a once in a lifetime statement. It also has a peculiarly Shi'ite form, in which the statement ''Ali is the friend of God' is added to the bipart Sunni formulation.[5]

History of the formula

The two basic statements of the *shahada* are found in the Qur'an but are not put together as a single statement, nor are they suggested in that book as being some sort of defining notion of what a Muslim is, as is implied within the concept of their ritual use. The refrain, 'There is no god but God' and variations upon it, are frequent in the scripture, found for example in Qur'an 47/19; 'Muhammad is the messenger of God' and statements to that effect are found also, for example in Qur'an 48/29, but the sense is never one of a refrain but rather as a part of an argument.

The emergence of the statement as a key part of Muslim identity is witnessed on coins from the first Muslim century and in the Dome of the Rock inscriptions, as well as in the *hadith* literature.

Coins from the eighth decade of the *hijri* calendar contain phrases such as 'There is no god but God alone', a statement reminiscent of Qur'an 5/73 and similar passages, but obviously it is differentiated by the addition of the word *wahid*, 'alone', from the first half of the *shahada*. 'Muhammad is the messenger of God' also appears starting, it would seem, with coins from the years 77 and 78 to which is added 'whom He sent with guidance and the religion of truth, that He might make it victorious over all religions'.[6] Such invocations continue on many coins from this point on and thus become the standard numismatic phraseology. It would appear to be an accident of history that coins continue to use a formula which does not precisely follow the *shahada* as might have been expected; this occurred because coinage was introduced apparently before the *shahada* reached its mature formulation. So, while the phrases of the *shahada* themselves became stock items of the religious vocabulary, it is apparent that, by the time of the issuance of these early coins, the phrases had not yet emerged as the ritual statement which was to identify all Muslims. However, it would appear to be a short step, both historically and phraseologically, before just that occurred.

The same comments hold for the Dome of the Rock inscriptions of 'Abd al-Malik as they do for the coins. Both phrases in reference to God and Muhammad are found in the inscriptions but they are found neither joined together nor distinguished as isolated elements within the texts.

For example, there is the statement on the outside of the colonnade on the south side: 'There is no god but God alone; He has no partner with Him' followed by 'Muhammad is the messenger of God'. Over the north door, the inscription reads 'Muhammad is the servant of God and His messenger whom He sent with the guidance and the religion of truth', the same as coins from Umayyad times after 'Abd al-Malik; the lack of emphasis on the formula expressions of later Islam is once again notable and significant for what it reveals of the gradual development of this element of Muslim identity.

As was mentioned earlier, the idea of the 'five pillars' is found listed in the *hadith* collection of Muslim ibn al-Hajjaj for example, but several of these reports indicate an instability in the matter of the *shahada*. While all the reports confirm that testifying to faith in one way or another was the first part of the 'five' elements stipulated by Muhammad, it is expressed in a number of ways: for example, it is called 'declaring the oneness of God' in one instance.[7] Furthermore, the actual form of the *shahada* witnessed in Muslim ibn al-Hajjaj is specifically a testimony to faith; that is, it is prefaced by the statement *shahada an*, 'the witness to faith is that'. The statement is, in fact, a part of the ritual prayer (and so the traditions themselves also come within the chapter concerned with the 'testimony in prayer'). The fact that the material as presented by Muslim ibn al-Hajjaj provides an uncohesive picture suggests two things: that the isolation of the *shahada* as an individual part of a concept of the 'five pillars' took place at least two centuries after Muhammad and that it was a formulation which received its final shape fairly late also.

Islamic prayer

Prayer, *salat*, is spoken of numerous times in the Qur'an; the notion of regular times of prayer is stipulated on some occasions but the text itself can only be made to support the classical Islamic practice of five prayers a day by a tenuous interpretation. Various elements of the ritual connected with the *salat* are also stipulated in the Qur'an, including standing, bowing, prostrating, facing in a set direction known as the *qibla* (the word itself is used in the Qur'an seven times, mainly in Qur'an 2/142–5), performing ablutions before prayer (Qur'an 5/6); the Friday (noon) prayer as one for the whole community is also designated in Qur'an 62/9. The recitation of the Qur'an within the prayer is also sometimes seen to be supported by the text itself (Qur'an 17/78, where reference is made to 'reading at daybreak'). None of these elements, however, is presented in a systematic or detailed manner such that one could actually reconstruct a ritual on the basis of these texts alone. Rather, most are presented in a very general manner (for example, Qur'an 25/63–4: *and the Mercy-giving's servants . . . who spend the night bowing down on their knees and standing before their Lord*) and only later did Muslims peg upon these verses the elaborate ritual which had developed in its own way and according to many different impulses.

By the time the collections of *hadith* material emerged, the ritual of the prayer had become quite explicit, although still not with total unanimity in detail. Such differences are to be found manifested in the traditions of the various schools of law, as with all the rituals in Islam, and therefore it is not possible to present a single picture of 'prayer' within Islam. Basic elements are common to all schools, however, and may be summarized.

The five times of prayer (*miqat*) are defined as daybreak (*salat al-subh* or *fajr*), noon (*salat al-zuhr*), midafternoon (*salat al-'asr*), sunset (*salat al-maghrib*) and evening (*salat al-'isha'* or *'atama*) but the precise way in which these times are determined varies. Clearly, it also depends upon where in the world the individual is at a given moment, so Muslims are, in theory, praying all over the world all the time. The call to prayer (*adhan*) is given by the muezzin (*mu'adhdhin*) at each mosque (*masjid*, literally 'the place of prostration' but in the Qur'an meaning 'sanctuary') but it is not necessary to go there in order to pray, except for the Friday noon prayer, for anyone may pray in any clean spot alone or in the company of others. Following the ablution, either minor (*wudu'*) or major (*ghusl*) depending on the state of ritual purity of the individual prior to the ablution, a series of recitations and body movements are undertaken in stages, many of which are liable to be supplemented by other traditional elements which vary according to the school of law. The prayer is done facing the direction of the Ka'ba in Mecca and entails recitation of sections of the Qur'an, with a special emphasis falling on *sura* 1, taking the worshipper from a standing position to one of bowing, half-sitting and full prostration. The whole sequence of the ritual is repeated twice in the morning, three times at sunset and four times in the noon, afternoon and evening prayers.[8]

The stipulation of these five prayer times is, according to Muslim tradition, a result of instructions given to Muhammad while on his heavenly journey. Clearly, even on the basis of the text of the Qur'an alone, the idea of there being five prayers took some time to emerge, but the evidence which is available to us just does not allow any insight into when the number five was decided upon or why. The suggestion that five is the median number between the three daily prayers of Judaism and the seven stages of the day of the Syrian Christian monastic orders fits within much of the elaboration of Muslim ritual as a conscious attempt to produce a self-definition which was mid-way between and yet clearly distinct from Judaism and Christianity.[9]

Friday noon prayer

While the daily prayer may be said anywhere and may be said alone (although saying it with others is considered more meritorious), the Friday noon prayer is held in a large *jami'* or 'congregational' mosque.[10] These buildings are generally supported by government funds, as opposed to the smaller mosques found throughout the Muslim world which have been built with private funds and are typically used by a defined group of people for the prayer at all other times. The Friday noon prayer will always be led by an *imam*, the prayer leader (such a person may be present any time a group of Muslims prays together, however, simply to keep the group in unison), and a sermon will be given by the *khatib* (who may be the same person as the *imam*).

Attendance at the Friday noon prayer was declared obligatory for all Muslims who were legally capable, with the exception of 'women, slaves, the sick, travellers, those tending the sick and those fleeing oppression', according to al-Baghdadi.[11]

Function of prayer

Additional prayers of a non-compulsory nature, but still of the ritualized *salat*-type, are also stipulated in Islam. Special prominence is given to the *witr* prayer, performed at night and to which an extra section, *rak'a*, may be added. Additional sections may also be added to the five daily prayers. As well, there is also the *wird*, the ritualized private prayer which concentrates on the recitation of the Qur'an. Another prayer is the *du'a*, a non-ritualized individual address to God. Prayer is not therefore restricted to the daily five prayers alone but may be performed on other occasions as the need and desire arises within the individual Muslim. Thus prayer as a phenomenon in Islam does not function simply to bring the community together at regular times of the day and the week; neither is it just a matter of providing structured time periods within the day to Muslim society, nor a way of simply providing a constant reminder of the presence of Islam in the world. Certainly it is all those things but it also does seem to be conceived as a personal communication with God, providing the opportunity for expressions of thankfulness and worship in the full sense of those words.

The mosque

Even though it is not actually necessary for the ritual of prayer, the mosque has become the central element manifesting the physical presence of Muslims in a given place in the world, a source of identity for those individual believers and a symbol and centre of purity for the Muslim community. The central elements of this physical manifestation of Muslim identity as connected to the mosque may be isolated and, as such, may well provide a statement of the symbols which Muslims feel essential to their self-definition and self-understanding as Muslims. The phenomenon of churches turned into mosques provides an interesting exposition of such elements. The most obvious examples which allow an insight into this conversion are those found in Istanbul which, while their transformation dates from a late period (the Turkish conquest of Constantinople was in 1453 and thus all such examples are necessarily after that date), include features which are fully representative of classical Muslim self-understanding.

Although overgrown and derelict in the 1980s and suffering from the effects of a partially completed restoration in 1964–5, the church identified as the Myrelaion and known as the Bodrum Camii or the Masih Ali Pasa mosque in Istanbul, provides a splendid example. Built in about 922, it is a building fascinating in its own right for its architectural design and the presence of a crypt underneath the building. In the late fifteenth or early sixteenth century, the church was converted into a mosque. The most obvious evidence of the conversion is the presence of the minaret, built into the south-west corner. The history of the minaret as a form of Muslim architecture is intriguing and, while its practical function of providing a place for the call to prayer is well known and often suggested to be the origin of the edifice, it seems more likely that the form was taken over from earlier buildings. The earliest examples of minarets are those found on the Mosque of al-Walid in Damascus constructed between 706 and 715; this mosque was built on the base of a Roman temple and incorporated the three original corner towers as 'minarets'. (The absence of a minaret on the Dome of the Rock should be noted.) The generalized symbolism of the minaret in the early period is not hard to comprehend: towering over the inhabitants is the pillar of the conquerors. It is clear, however, that regardless of its early function, in classical Islam a minaret became the central symbol of both the Muslim faith and the place of worship[12] as illustrated in the conversion process of churches into mosques. In the Myrelaion, no other major architectural modifications were required to make the church functional as a mosque. A small window appears to have been installed on the ground level to allow sufficient light for Qur'an reading. The other changes are all internal and to do with furnishings. A *mihrab*, or niche, indicating the direction of prayer, was provided. This indicator would appear to be a necessary feature of converted buildings but a purpose-built mosque would, of course, be properly aligned anyway and thus it appears redundant in such instances. Yet the niche is found in all mosques; it may be that the feature was copied from the design of ancient religious buildings, being the place designated for the presence of the honoured image in Roman temples, for example.[13] A *minbar*, or pulpit, was required for the sermon (*khutba*) of the preacher (*khatib*). A women's gallery had to be installed to keep the sexes separate. All these items had to be aligned in the correct Muslim direction, facing Mecca, within the former church structure. Ancillary chambers appear to have been constructed for the *imam* and the muezzin, and a vestibule created for latecomers. No evidence of a place for ablutions appears to exist, although the presence of a cistern within the original building complex may have provided a source for the necessary flowing water.

This pattern of conversion may be witnessed many times over in Istanbul and in many other parts of the Islamic world. Istanbul provides a further vivid example in the church of SS Sergius and Bacchus built in 527 for Justinian and thus older than Haghia Sophia, which, with its four minarets provides another instance of a conversion. Some churches proved more problematic, as in what is believed to be the Church of St Andrew in Krisei, now known as the Koca Mustafa Pasa Camii, which required a complete reorientation for its successful use as a mosque.

Muslim charity

Alms-tax, *zakat* (the term *sadaqa* is often synonymous but can also mean 'freewill offerings'), like prayer with which it is often mentioned in tandem, is demanded in the Qur'an in statements which provide exhortations to believers to give (*You will never attain virtue until you spend something you are fond of*, says Qur'an 3/92), but few details are actually provided as to what to give and when. The Qur'an responds to a demand to know how much to give in *sura* 2/219 with the statement *As much as you can spare!* An explicit statement is made about the recipients of the alms, with the result that Qur'an 9/60 has served as the peg for all legal discussions on the issue. *Charity is {meant} only for the poor, the needy, those working at {collecting and distributing} it, those {possible converts} whose hearts are being reconciled {to yours}, for freeing captives and debtors, and in {striving along} God's way, and for the wayfarer, as a duty imposed by God.* A general emphasis throughout the Qur'an is made on helping the poor, orphans and widows. It is also suggested that all such payments should be made discreetly, without drawing attention to the one who is giving. The alms-tax given should come out of the money or produce which one possesses.

The system of zakat

It was up to the jurists of the later centuries to develop a precise system of donation and payment. This development can be seen in the books of *hadith*, and the institution of charity provided endless opportunity for the jurists to work out subtle details and theoretical considerations.

Early *hadith* reports appear to be ignorant of precisely how much should be given as *zakat* and from precisely what sorts of things it should be paid; such reports simply say that possessing 'wealth' is forbidden and thus everything which is in excess should be given away. Within the developed schools of law, however, full rules emerged which, while they vary in precise detail from school to school, can be summarized fairly accurately. Crops of the field, grapes and dates are liable to *zakat* on each crop, at an amount stipulated as 10 per cent of the crop, paid at harvest time. Camels, oxen and other small domestic animals which are freely grazing are also liable, the amount paid being a portion of the excess over certain stipulated amounts. Of gold, silver and merchandise, 2½ per cent of the amount held each year is also payable. The amount is payable directly to the recipients but it is preferred that the tax be paid to the authorities in charge of its distribution (a notion seen to be supported by the fact that the Qur'an refers to those involved in collecting *zakat* as one of the groups eligible to receive it). In practice, *zakat* became difficult to collect especially in times of high taxation. At various times during Muslim history, however, governments inspired by pious scholars attempted to return to a system of collecting *zakat* as the only legitimate form of taxation. But the amount collected often proved insufficient and eventually there occurred a reversion to other forms of tax on items more profitable to the government which were not covered in the traditional working out of the *zakat* laws (for example, by the imposition of import duties).

Zakat has shown great flexibility over time in adapting to and being adapted by social and political realities. For example, variation in whether the tax was a voluntary one or a required contribution to the state frequently reflected the conditions at the time in terms of the state's prosperity. Also, the imposition of *zakat* was seen, starting about the eleventh century, as the central symbol of the revival of Islamic rule; the 'proper' (that is, the juridical) implementation of the tax was urged by reformers and initiated by rulers at various points in history in order to bolster Islamic ideological claims. Attempts by al-Malik al-Kamil (d. 1238), a ruler in the Ayyubid dynasty centred in Egypt, invoked the Islamic ideal of voluntary payment of taxes under the term *zakat* but the programme quickly crumbled under the impact of the revenue lost by the central government.[14]

The Muslim fast

During the ninth month of the *hijri* calendar, Ramadan, a fast is enjoined upon Muslims. From sunrise to just after sunset for the thirty days of this month of the lunar calendar, adults are ordered to abstain from all food and drink (the regulation being not to allow any material substance to enter the body in so far as that is possible), from deliberate vomiting and from having sexual intercourse or emission of semen if that is a result of conscious desire. Menstruation, bleeding after child birth, an unsound mind or intoxication produce an invalid fast. Numerous legal qualifications surround the fast, including what to do if the fast is violated and what sorts of behaviour in general are permissable during the month; the various schools of law see different implications arising from many of the situations.

It is considered especially meritorious to read the whole of the Qur'an during the month of Ramadan. To facilitate this, the text has been divided into 30 equal sections, one for each day of the month. When the fasting month is over, the *'id al-fitr* celebration is held; this is the major festival of the Muslim year. The day itself sees a special public prayer for the whole community and following that, a vast feast is put on, with celebration, visiting and giving of gifts (called the *zakat al-fitr*) being special features.

The Qur'an contains several fairly detailed explanations of the fast of Ramadan, indicating that it was a practice which came into existence early in Islam, being recognised as a symbol of the religion or at least indicating Islam's comparability to Judaism and Christianity. As the Qur'an itself declares in *sura* 2/183, *You who believe, fasting has been prescribed for you just as it was prescribed for those before you, so that you may do your duty.* The sense is, therefore, that Islam has a practice equivalent to that of Judaism and Christianity, although it is distinct in its calendar situation and length: *The month of Ramadan is when the Qur'an was sent down as a guidance for mankind, and with explanations for guidance, and as a Standard. Let any of you who is at home during the month, fast in it* (Qur'an 2/185). Here we have a case of a ritual which is adopted and adapted from the earlier religions but which is given a distinctly Islamic flavour and mythological significance with the month's connection to the revelation of the Qur'an.[15]

Stories abound in the *hadith* material concerning an 'earlier' fast which Muhammad instituted on the Jewish Day of Atonement. Suggested to have been a one day, twenty-four hour fast, the reports are often seen to be an explanation of the Qur'anic phrase suggesting that there was an earlier fast (that is, Qur'an 2/183, quoted above); as such, the historical value of the reports is certainly questionable. Most notable, however, is the understanding that these reports provide for the significance of Ramadan; the month-long fast is to be understood as the truly Islamic version of the institution of fasting.

Fasting at times other than Ramadan

Fasting in Islam is undertaken more often than simply during Ramadan. The notion of *kaffara*, atonement for sin or for duties which have been omitted, is stipulated in the Qur'an on a number of occasions: in *sura* 2/196, fasting is to replace the pilgrimage for those unable to go to Mecca under certain conditions; in Qur'an 4/92, fasting is an atonement for killing a believer by mistake; in Qur'an 5/89, fasting is prescribed for breaking an oath; in Qur'an 5/95, fasting is the penalty for killing an animal while on the *hajj*; and in Qur'an 58/4, one may fast in order to retract a divorce. In each of these situations, fasting is seen as a replacement or another possibility in the suggested ways of making amends for one's moral or ritual errors. All these indicate that fasting as an activity in general is seen to have a certain sense of redemptive effect within Islam; this redemption is sometimes thought to be applicable to the fasting which takes place in the month of Ramadan as well, at least in a limited way.

The Muslim pilgrimage

The *hajj* to Mecca and its surrounding area is a ritual lasting up to seven days which contains within it a fully detailed sequence of events enjoined upon all those who are physically able to come to the city. Performed during the first half of the last month of the year, Dhu'l-Hijja, the *hajj* requires a state of ritual purity for the activities. Prior to the *hajj* itself, ritual purification is undertaken and the Ka'ba is circumambulated and a run is performed between al-Safa and al-Marwa, two hillocks near the Ka'ba (now joined to the central Meccan mosque by a covered arcade); both activities are performed seven times, interspersed with prayers and invocations. On the seventh of Dhu'l-Hijja, the pilgrimage itself actually starts, with a ritual purification and a prayer service at the mosque around the Ka'ba. Over the next three days, the following activities take place. The pilgrims assemble in Mina, just outside Mecca, and stay there for the night. The next morning they depart for the plain of 'Arafat, 15 kilometres east, and assemble on the Mount of Mercy where a prayer ritual is performed and a ceremony entitled the 'standing' is undertaken, lasting from the time the sun passes the meridian until sunset. That evening, the pilgrims return to Muzdalifa, about half-way back to Mina, where the night is spent. The next day a journey to Mina brings them to the stone pillar (*jamrat al-'aqaba*) at which seven pebbles are thrown; the column is said to represent Satan. This is followed by a ritual slaughter of sheep, goats and camels and a meal, the *'id al-adha*, 'the festival of the sacrifice' (performed by all Muslims whether in Mecca or not and seen as the second major festival of Islam). Returning to Mecca, the Ka'ba is circumambulated and the running between al-Safa and al-Marwa (unless completed prior to the *hajj* itself) is performed.[16] The state of ritual purity is also abandoned on this day, symbolized by men having their heads shaved and women having a lock of hair cut off. Three days of celebration at Mina generally follow for most pilgrims, with more stones thrown at the three pillars of Satan, all followed by another circumambulation of the Ka'ba. A visit to Medina will also often be included before the pilgrims return to their own homes.[17]

The Qur'an's major testimony to this ritual is found in *sura* 2/196–200 and *sura* 5/95–7. Various parts of the ritual are detailed, as are some of the legal regulations which bear on the participants. No full and cohesive explanation is given, however.

An element which does receive mention on a number of occasions is the relationship of some elements of the pilgrimage to the activities of Abraham and Ishmael. The Qur'an states in *sura* 2/127 that Abraham and Ishmael *laid the foundations for the House* [understood as the Ka'ba] and that they did a number of the activities which the later pilgrims also do: performed the circumambulation, ran between al-Safa and al-Marwa, sacrificed a sheep and stoned Satan.

Historically, the pilgrimage has given tremendous prominence to Mecca but, as has already been mentioned in chapter 4 above, there was a time when Jerusalem may well have been an alternative pilgrimage destination, although clearly the Dome of the Rock was not constructed with a view to facilitating the vast number of pilgrims which are received at Mecca each year. Notably the inscriptions in the Dome do not exhort people to perform a pilgrimage; the inscriptions are there, however, in order to be read while performing a circumambulatory ritual within the domed area.

Other ritual activities

The extent to which Muslim identity is expressed through ritual is not limited to the 'five pillars', although the prominence of that grouping is obviously high. The *mawlid* festival, celebrating the birth of Muhammad (not fully established in Islam until about the thirteenth century) and the informal *du'a* prayers are two additional ritual-type activities which are considered by Muslims to be significant in terms of the expression of their faith. Visits to tombs of holy men and women are also a popular activity, especially in areas which have been deeply affected by the mystical side of Islam. Such visits are generally used as occasions either to ask for favours of the deceased saint or to ask for forgiveness. The power of the saint is believed to reside in his or her ability to intercede on behalf of the individual believer with God.

Among Shi'ites, ceremonies connected to the tenth day of the first month of the year, Muharram, play a prominent role and give the Shi'ites a special external manifestation of their identity over-against the Sunni community. Known as the festival of 'Ashura', the activities on this day are pictured in terms of recreating historical events from the early history of the Shi'ite movement connected especially to 'Ali's son Husayn. Martyrdom for the faith of Islam is the central motif along with a celebration of the special character of the family of 'Ali. While slight differences may manifest themselves in other Muslim rituals as performed by the Shi'ites, such are no greater than the variations between the Sunni schools of law on similar issues. What differences do exist, however, have gained symbolic value for the Shi'ites in terms of providing a distinct (and, implicitly, correct) religious identity, especially in times of political antagonism with the Sunni world.[18]

The interpretation of Muslim ritual

Most noticeable when contemplating the sum of Muslim ritual is the emphasis upon the ritualism of the activities; all events are fully planned and formalized. But beyond that, one may observe a general lack of mythological sense in any of the rituals. The only meaning which can be seen in these rituals, according to many classical Muslim thinkers and modern scholars of Islam alike, is their sense of being an expression of an individual's piety and obedience to God's command and as an indication of the person's membership within the Islamic community. There is a very real sense of what has been termed 'anti-sacramentalism' and also of the rituals being 'commemorative' but at the same time 'amythical';[19] that is, many of the actions in these rituals are done with a remembrance of past actions of Muhammad or Abraham, but without those actions becoming mythological, such that the believer becomes, in any sense, the person of the past, for example. Likewise, the sacrifice of the *hajj* and the performance of the fast of Ramadan for the most part do not take on the character of sacraments, conceived to have specific effects for the believer, but rather remain acts which individuals do within their sense of obedience. Overall, it has been suggested that ritual is the full manifestation of the special character of Islam, separate from other religions by its conscious decision to be unique in its ritual constituents; that process of creating a separate definition appears to have been done, in the case of the development of the ritual practices, in a reasonably arbitrary fashion with no overall consistent pattern imposed in creating that 'uniqueness' of Islam within the Judeo-Christian milieu. Islam, in its construction of its rituals, is different from Judaism and Christianity and has rejected, or at least greatly modified, the central ritual activities of its two predecessors. In this way, it has created its 'uniqueness' through difference, but that does remains a 'uniqueness' which cannot be systematized into a cohesive perspective, at least not within the framework of ritual.

PART THREE

Alternative visions of Islamic identity

CHAPTER EIGHT

Shi'ism

Sectarianism in Islam

For the most part, Islam remained remarkably unified in its religious manifestations during the classical period. Only the splits between the legal and theological schools already discussed and the creation of the Shi'a of 'Ali, or simply the Shi'ites, have produced any degree of cleavage and only the latter has produced a true sense of an 'alternative vision' of Islam.

A number of treatises were written by various Muslim authors which detailed a tendency toward sectarianism within the faith which would seem to contradict the above statement. Famous works by al-Baghdadi (d. 1037) and al-Shahrastani (d. 1153) provide lists of the 73 'groups' into which the Islamic community fractured. These works, however, reflect less what would normally be considered true variation in expression of Islamic identity, but more a documentation of variations on specific points of Muslim theology. The books are a part of a tendency towards classification of all sorts of sundry matters which was common in classical Islamic times, but they do also reflect an interpretation and justification of a tradition ascribed to Muhammad which speaks of his community dividing into 73 (or 71 or 72) parts; the important concluding statement of the tradition provides its significance: only one of these groups will actually be saved in the hereafter. It was the job of the authors of these texts, then, to enumerate the multiplicity of groups, while, at the same time, providing a clear definition of the group which will be saved, that group, of course, being identical with the author's own allegiances. In some instances, one suspects that in these books political rebels have been made into theologically-based heretics, thus once again reinforcing the traditional picture of a well-defined 'Islam' as existing from the very earliest times.[1]

One of the groups detailed by these 'heresiographers', a group divided into numerous sub-divisions according to their classificatory schemes, was the Shi'a of 'Ali. Once again, how many of these groups really existed as clearly identified units is questionable and certainly few of them actually survived for any substantial period of time. Several main groupings did become prominent, however.

Shi'ism's understanding of its origins

As was mentioned in the discussion of the rise of theology, Shi'ism pictures its roots back in the days of 'Ali ibn abi Talib and the early caliphs. The Shi'a, or 'party', of 'Ali were those who defended his right to rule the early community in the civil war with Mu'awiya. They claimed, on the basis of statements of Muhammad and by virtue of 'Ali's relationship to Muhammad (being his cousin and son-in-law), that he had a legitimate claim to rule. Much is made of traditions from Muhammad, accepted by both the Sunnis and Shi'ites, in which 'Ali is designated as having a special relationship to Muhammad; al-Tirmidhi (author of one of the canonical Sunni books of *hadith*) reports: 'The prophet said in reply to someone who had complained about 'Ali: "What do you think of one who loves God and his prophet and who in turn is loved by God and his prophet?"' Also transmitted is 'The most loved of women to the prophet of God is Fatima ['Ali's wife, Muhammad's daughter] and the most loved of men is 'Ali.'[2] Such traditions, however, tend to fall into a general category of discussion of the 'merits of the companions' found in all *hadith* literature, in which each of the early followers of Islam is honoured. In this way, their authority as 'founding fathers' and subsequently as transmitters of *hadith* was enhanced and it seems likely that this was the function of such reports in the beginning; it was only when 'Ali as an individual had his persona enhanced by the Shi'ites that such reports took upon themselves a greater significance. It would appear, however, that this must have taken place to a great extent after traditions enhancing 'Ali's position were already in circulation in the early community; 'Ali's position within the family of Muhammad is probably sufficient to explain why early sources would consider him an especially prominent person.

From the Shi'ite perspective there was more at stake in the whole debate, however, for example concerning the nature of the rule of the early community. Was the leader to be one who combined religious with political authority? Or, with the death of Muhammad, had religious authority passed to each individual believing Muslim? It remains a matter of debate among many scholars as to whether or not 'Ali received his earliest support because of a nascent belief in his religious significance and thus his authority in religious matters, and how that nature was to be understood – an element developed fully in later Shi'ism, as we shall see – or whether this was a purely political manoeuvre which later became coloured with religious significance.

However, as was the case for theology, these debates among scholars essentially accept the Muslim accounts at their face value and argue over the various aspects of them, rather than appreciating the ideological viewpoint from which such material was compiled. These debates still work from the standpoint of acceptance of the data provided about the early period and those data's impulse to demonstrate a legitimating and detailed view of Islamic origins.

The Shi'a and the Qur'an

Most significant in the stance of the Shi'ites, *vis-à-vis* their origins, is their general acceptance of the text of the Qur'an virtually intact, in line with the Sunnis. While there certainly have been tendencies within the Shi'ite community to debate the accuracy of the text as they have it and even a tendency to suggest modifications to the text – citing additions, omissions, changes and alterations to the version promulgated by 'Uthman – this sort of activity has been relatively restrained. Much of the contemplated modification to the Qur'anic text is of such a nature as to take place within the legitimated (from the Sunni perspective) range of 'variant readings'; an example of this is found in Qur'an 3/110, *You are the best community which has been produced for mankind*, such that, rather than being read *umma*, 'community', Shi'ites have read the word as *a'imma* and taken as referring to the leaders of the Shi'ite community, the Imams. What all this may be taken to suggest is that the differentiation between Sunni and Shi'ite arose only after the promulgation of an established text of the Qur'an.

This view of the historical development of Sunnis and Shi'ites fits in with the account of the rise of Islam and the caliph's authority given earlier in this book. A fully variant text of the Qur'an in the hands of the Shi'ites would have indicated an earlier establishment of Shi'ism than the evidence concerning the rise of Islam as a whole might otherwise suggest. It might also have suggested a 'fixed' text of the Qur'an being established early on, to which the Shi'ites responded with their own version. However, since the Shi'ites do *not* have their own Qur'an, both the late establishment of Shi'ism and Sunnism as two interpretations of Islam, and the establishment of a fully fixed text of the Qur'an prior to that division are historically possible.

The Shi'ites and hadith

The other significant element in understanding the rise of Shi'ism is the observation that the Shi'ites have a distinct body of *hadith* material, much of it traced back to or through the early leaders of the Shi'ite community or, at the very least, containing variants compared to the Sunni community's versions.[3] In its written form, this material started to emerge during the ninth century. Given the function of the *hadith* in Islam in general, the existence of a separate body of material indicates that the central matter of dispute causing the separation of Sunnism and Shi'ism was one of ultimate authority in the community as a whole and within each group separately. In the early unified community, the caliph appears to have had complete authority, as was discussed in chapter 4 above. With the rise of the learned classes in the eighth century, the disputes over authority became more pronounced; the Sunni community with its trust placed in fixed written sources of authority emerged, leaving what became the Shi'ite group continuing to hold to authority vested in an individual.

The authority of the Shi'ite Imam

This understanding of the development of authority makes sense of what is the most prominent and distinct element in Shi'ism and that is the person of the Imam. Designated by Muhammad, 'Ali was the first Imam for the Shi'ites; this was seen as the designation of a spiritual position, not one of temporal power, and thus the inability of the Imams in later times to seize power within the community was of no particular concern to their followers. The function of the Imam was to guide his followers by explaining and clarifying the divine law but also to direct those believers in the inner spiritual path of Islam. This he was able to do because of his close connection to God, facilitated by *ilham*, 'inspiration', (as distinct from *wahy*, 'revelation' which is the mode through which scripture is produced) and the knowledge passed on to him by the one who designated him. God's mercy and justice indicate that there can never be a time when the world is without an Imam, for if that were so, people would have no guidance and there would be no proof available of God's beneficence towards His creation. The Imam is thus termed the *hujja*, 'proof' and *hadi*, 'guide'. The persons who were to be Imams were designated by God from the beginning of creation, and were even viewed as pre-existent in the form of primordial light according to some mystically flavoured interpretations. They are, as a consequence of these ideas, seen as sinless and the best of all creation. The actual existence of an Imam is to be taken as part of God's beneficence towards humanity, for he facilitates the salvation of God's creation by providing a sure guide in the world and a certain answer to issues of dispute.

The most prominent branch of Shi'ism, known as the 'Twelvers' (in Arabic *Ithna 'ashariyya*) or more generically as the Imamis, identifies a chain of twelve persons through whom the line of authority passed in the formative centuries of Islam. These people were designated by their predecessors and their birth was generally pictured as accompanied by various miraculous signs, confirming this designation. That the clear delineation of this line was, up to a certain point, *ex post facto* would appear likely and is even evidenced by mid-tenth century Shi'ite sources who speak of people in their community being unsure of the identity of the Imam; it will only have been when the need for authority emerged within the community that the tracing back of a chain of authority (as in the *isnad* of a *hadith*) would have actually been necessary. The established line of the twelve Imams is as follows:

'Ali ibn abi Talib, d. 661
Hasan, 'Ali's son, d. 669
Husayn, 'Ali's second son, d. 680
Zayn al-'Abidin, Husayn's son, d. 712 or 713
Muhammad al-Baqir, Zayn's son, d. 735 (?)
Ja'far al-Sadiq, Muhammad's son, d. 765
Musa al-Kazim, Ja'far's son, d. 799
'Ali al-Rida, Musa's son, d. 818
Muhammad al-Taqi al-Jawad, 'Ali's son, d. 835
'Ali al-Hadi, Muhammad's son, d. 868
Hasan al-'Askari, 'Ali's son, d. 873 or 874
Muhammad al-Mahdi, Hasan's son, born 868

The formation of Shi'ism

Ja'far al-Sadiq appears to have been the pivotal figure through whom Shi'ism actually came into existence as a religious movement. Up to that point, the best that one may suppose is that rival groups, whose primary focus was in the political arena, existed in the community; some of these groups saw their right to rule traced back to 'Ali. As with the emergence of the whole system of Islam itself, the particular elements manifested in Shi'ism took time to evolve, even though the sources themselves wish to project the origins back to the earliest period. The rise of the 'Abbasid caliphate making its appeal to persons in sympathy with the rights of 'Ali, would coincide with the dates of Ja'far al-Sadiq. It is with the sixth Imam and his designated successor Musa al-Kazim that the incipient notions of the imamate would appear to have originated, based on the information provided by various heresiographical works and Shi'ite tradition itself, which sees Ja'far as the formative spokesman. Crucial elements here are the procedure for the designation of the Imam (rather than that person being determined by a process of battle – the Shi'ite platform can then defend a quietist attitude despite a lineage which would suggest a need to usurp rule in the world; this also had the effect of cutting off a tendency towards proliferation of rival claimants to the position of Imam) and the Imam's receipt of esoteric knowledge passed on from the previous Imam. Be this as it may, it is only in the time of the twelfth Imam that we actually have any Shi'ite sources which provide us with detailed information on the Shi'a and their beliefs and it is clear that it is in the period after the twelfth Imam that Shi'ism as we know it today actually came into being.

The occultation of the last Imam

The twelfth Imam is said to have disappeared, and to have entered into his 'lesser occultation', being hidden from the view of the world. He designated a series of four persons (in parallel to the first four caliphs perhaps) to whom he communicated his commands; this situation lasted from 874 until 941. He then entered into his 'greater occultation', in which condition he no longer communicates with the world. This notion of occultation is a necessary consequence of the line of Imams ending at a particular point in history; if humanity cannot be without an Imam and the line of Imams has ended, then the last Imam cannot be dead but must be alive – or else a substitute for him must exist. Known as the *ghayba*, the occultation will last until God determines its end. The return of the twelfth Imam is awaited, with him in the role of the messianic Mahdi; this will occur shortly before the day of judgement. At that time, he will be manifested on earth and will lead the righteous into battle against the forces of evil; finally, good will triumph over evil and the Imam will subsequently rule over the world in a period of peace.[4]

The notion that there should be 12 Imams and that the twelfth should permanently 'disappear' took some time to solidify within Shi'ism. Certainly authors writing at the time of the twelfth Imam appeared to have expected the line to continue beyond him; although they admitted that at the time he was 'hiding', he was clearly expected to show himself once again. Indeed, the presence of the Imam as a 'proof' and a 'guidance' was deemed essential and was the major element in polemic against the Sunni schools, whom the Shi'ites felt were adrift with no guidance. It would appear to be the case, however, that other Shi'ite groups had already developed the notions of a limited chain of Imams and of the last one 'disappearing'; all that was really happening, then, was that the Imami group was employing already circulating ideas as an explanation of events taking place in their 'twelver-Shi'i' line. By the time of the Shi'ite writer al-Kulayni in the tenth century, the idea of there being a line of 12 Imams was established, although for the rest of the century, authors still found it necessary to compose works which would explain and defend this notion of an occulted Imam. Arguments in favour of there being a line of only 12 Imams were found in Qur'anic references to the number 12 (e.g. 12 months in the year, Qur'an 9/36) and in Shi'ite and Sunni traditions which talk of Muhammad naming 12 successors. These are found in Sunni sources written in a period before the occultation of the twelfth Imam and perhaps reflect notions regarding '12' as a number symbolic of restoration, fulfilment, and authority, as in the 12 tribes of Israel and the 12 disciples of Jesus.[5]

There seem to be political reasons lying behind the idea of the 'disappearance' of the twelfth Imam which account for it becoming a successful doctrine in Shi'ite circles. As long as the Imam was physically present in the world, he represented a threat, albeit ineffectual, to the ruling powers. The Shi'ites found themselves virtually always persecuted under the rule of the 'Abbasids. Removing the worldly reality of the Imam, after enduring some 100 years of 'Abbasid rule, was a way of securing a continued existence for the group, but also may be linked to a growing sense of material prosperity among certain groups of Shi'ites which they were unwilling to forego.[6] Co-operation with the ruling powers was far easier without the Imam present, but believing in his 'occultation' meant that one's loyalty to him did not have to diminish; co-operation with the rulers brought power as well as a more comfortable existence, something which took place under the pro-Shi'ite Buwayhids and clearly separated political and religious dimensions of existence. The Shi'ite doctrine of *taqiyya* ('religious dissimulation'), by which it was considered acceptable to conceal one's true allegiance in the face of adversity, fitted in with this situation and attitude. It is likely also that, as with Sunni Islam, a rise in the status and power of the *'ulama'*, the scholarly classes, put pressure on the Imam whose actual presence proved inconvenient for the learned classes and their expectations and aspirations. Also for all practical purposes, by the time of the twelfth Imam, the *'ulama'* had taken over positions of effective authority anyway, the Imam himself generally being kept out of contact with the vast majority of his followers; it was dangerous for the Imam to be in public view, owing to his political pretensions. The authority of the learned classes after the *ghayba* rested on the basis of their knowledge of the traditions transmitted by the Imams. Thus the emergence of the books of *hadith* at approximately the time of the lesser occultation is to be expected.

Shi'ite theology

Much of developed Shi'ite theology follows that of the Mu'tazilites, discussed in chapter 5 above, with a few crucial differences. It is significant to note that, in a sense, Shi'ism represents a re-emergence of Mu'tazilite thought which appears to have lost much of its popular appeal in the Sunni world in the preceding century or so. The significance and meaning of the Imamate were the major factors which separated the Mu'tazilites and the Shi'ites. Further significant differences are really a consequence of this stance. One of the Imam's functions is to intercede on behalf of his followers in the hereafter; this function runs counter to the Mu'tazilite insistence on 'the punishment and the threat' as applying to all persons, consistent with their perception of the justice of God. Likewise, for the Shi'ites there can be no 'intermediate position', that of the hypocrite, applicable to those who appear to sin in their actions but declare their belief; those who declare their allegiance to the Imam are quite clearly members of the community and must be accepted as such.

Other than these elements, the theological doctrines are familiar: belief in divine unity and justice, in the role of prophethood and the bringing of the law by sinless prophets, and in the resurrection at the end of time.

The emergence of this theological position

The Shi'ites did not always hold this theological position, however; the debates in the post-*ghayba* period clearly show an evolution from a tradition-based system to a more fully rationalistic one. Prior to that however, in the very early period, the information regarding the situation is even less clear and provides at least some evidence of an even greater measure of shift in theological doctrine. However, the fact of the matter remains that there are no sources which can be trusted to be fully reliable to give us information on the doctrinal stance of the Shi'ites prior to the tenth century. Some scholars have made the suggestion that any sources internal to the group itself suffered destruction at the hands of later Shi'ites who found the early doctrines unacceptable. The degree to which these early doctrines were contrary to later ones is suggested, perhaps, by Sunni sources, specifically al-Khayyat (writing around 882) and al-Ash'ari (writing around 912). The doctrines of these early groups, dubbed the *ghulat*, 'the exaggerators', included notions of transmigration of souls, an anthropomorphic conception of God, God's willing of the evil deeds of humanity and the possibility of alteration in God's will. At one point it is also held that some believed in the absolute divine nature of the Imam, although the later Sunni sources perhaps reflect the lessening of this doctrine for they do not mention it. The trouble here is that the Sunni sources are clearly polemical in tone and approach and the items of doctrine with which the *ghulat* are associated are precisely those items which bring about the greatest reprobation from the Sunni schools; to represent these doctrines as being held by the largest Shi'ite school at the time may well be a case of attempting to deliberately mislead.

Ibn Babawayh

By the tenth century, when the Buwayhid dynasty took over in Baghdad and made the 'Abbasid caliph simply a tributary to the ruler, Shi'ism had become a political force and a clearer picture of its theological stance starts to emerge. Ibn Babawayh (d. 991) appears to have been one of the leading figures in this movement. He wrote against the notion of anthropomorphism – which certainly suggests that some Shi'ites still held to such doctrines – and, by the end of his life, he also seemed convinced that humanity has a degree of free will under God's law: 'Our belief concerning human actions is that they are created . . . in the sense that Allah possesses foreknowledge . . . and not in the sense that Allah compels mankind to act in a particular manner by creating a certain disposition. . . . And the meaning of this is that Allah has never ceased to be aware of the potentialities . . . of human beings'.[7] At an earlier stage of his life, however, he held to a firmer predestinarian position. What marks all of his works is a reliance on tradition rather than reason and a total rejection of the stance of *kalam* ('the partisans of the *kalam* will perish and the Muslims will be saved'[8]); this is similar to al-Ash'ari's stance in the Sunni world who was reacting to the full force of Mu'tazilite doctrine. Ibn Babawayh, on the other hand, came before the major impact of Mu'tazilite thought in Shi'ism, although some tendency in the direction of rationalism is to be noted in writers from earlier in the tenth century.

Later theologians

Mu'tazilite theology proper came into Shi'ism through the work of al-Shaykh al-Mufid (d. 1022), al-Sharif al-Murtada (d. 1044) and al-Tusi (d. 1067). While the basis for the particulars of the Mu'tazilite position was already firmly established in Shi'ism (and, some would say, had been so since the time of Ja'far al-Sadiq), it is these authors who emphasized the use of reason in support of the doctrine, seeing the need to defend the religion on that basis. Al-Shaykh al-Mufid argues for a less radical type of Mu'tazilite stance than some of the later authors; he avoids saying that people are the actual 'creators' of their own acts and that the Qur'an is created: rather, the Qur'an 'originated in time' and acts are 'produced' or 'made'. God's actions in the world are always in the best interests of humanity (this being provided as an explanation of evil in the world). Over all, al-Shaykh al-Mufid attempted to avoid going beyond what he sees as the limits of Qur'anic phraseology in talking of theology.[9]

With the later authors the position became more radical, with reason becoming the basis of all doctrine rather than being the tool by which authoritative doctrine could be defended and enhanced, as it was for al-Shaykh al-Mufid. Al-Murtada may best be thought of as the Shi'ite al-Ash'ari in the sense that his writings became the basis for all later Shi'ite exposition of theology, being the virtually unquestioned source.

Why the Shi'ites adopted this rationalist position in theology would appear to be connected to the need for authority. While the Imam was in the world, the source of authority for the Shi'ite community was clear: it was the Imam; being an authoritative source was the very purpose of his presence in the world. The Sunnis were, in the Shi'ite view, reduced to merely conjecturing on all elements of their religion. With the *ghayba* of the twelfth Imam, authority first came through the series of four representatives who were able to put questions to the Imam and bring back answers. With the greater occultation, however, this could no longer happen, although the appearance of the Imam to a worthy individual, either in reality or in a dream, was at least held to be possible. In the absence of the Imam, then, authority was in the hands of the learned classes. But this was no better than the Sunni position, which the Shi'ites had criticized for having no sound basis. Mu'tazilite theology provided a way around this problem by suggesting that reason alone could provide the certitude which is required; deduction based on reason, therefore, rather than tradition, as used by the Sunnis, was the ideal replacement for the Imam, whose rulings would only conform to the laws of reason anyway.

Shi'ite legal thought

In the legal field, a late development is also quite clear, as in theology. The tenth-century work by al-Kulayni, *al-Kafi fi 'ilm al-din* ('The Sufficient in the Knowledge of Religion'), marks a pivotal point in the emergence of defined Shi'ite law. This work gathers together traditions, either from the Imams or from Muhammad and transmitted through the Imams, which serve as the basis for all discussions (both legal and theological) in this period. The writing of the book is significant and contains, by its very composition, a polemical element. The book clearly wants to argue that the Imam in the world is no more: no longer can that source of authority be used, and the Shi'ites, like the Sunnis, must turn to written sources to substantiate their position. The writing of a work such as al-Kulayni's marks a stage in the emergence of Shi'ism in which the learned classes, who had control of the sources, were starting to assert their authority; in such a way, it was ensured that any potential claimants to the position of the Imam were effectively silenced. Al-Kulayni's book is one of the four, the others written by Ibn Babawayh and al-Tusi (the latter having two to his credit), which are considered the counterparts to the six authoritative collections of *hadith* in the Sunni world.

Without the Imam, or his representatives, in the world, the specific duties assigned to him were said to have lapsed. These included leading the holy war (*jihad*), division of booty of war, leading the Friday prayer, putting juridical decisions into effect, imposing legal penalties, and receiving the religious taxes.[10] The absence of the Imam left the community leaderless and it fell to al-Tusi in the eleventh century to enunciate a theory of juridical authority being in the hands of those knowledgeable in jurisprudence, the *fuqaha'*. Even then, the role of the jurists was limited and it took several centuries and a number of other theorists to develop a more encompassing theory; it was only in the sixteenth century that the *fuqaha'* took over all the duties of the occulted Imam, with the exception of offensive *jihad* which, it was determined, could only be undertaken by the Imam himself.[11]

The absoluteness of this delegation of the authority of the Imam was tempered by the theological speculation over the return of the twelfth Imam. This expected return, though, was of little practical concern to the jurists whose role was to create a legal system with no reference to a living Imam, only to one who existed theologically.[12]

Shi'ite legal practice

The theoretical development of the principles of Shi'ite jurisprudence was, for the most part, late in being written (fourteenth to sixteenth centuries), at least in comparison with Sunni development. To some extent, therefore, Shi'ism depended upon the principles already enunciated within Sunnism in order to develop the legal basis of their society; the differences between the two are, as a result, slight. Shi'ism in this view is little more than another legal school, parallel to the four major Sunni schools. Minor differences occur in the prayer ritual and the fast of Ramadan but these are precisely of a nature which would be seen as a variation between schools of law. Friday noon prayer is not as important to the Shi'ites because of the absence of the Imam who is supposed to lead that prayer, although this became a problem of some seriousness in juridical discussions. Various practices are enjoined such as visiting the tombs of the Imams and these visits are conducted with extensive rituals on a par with those of the *hajj*.

There are, of course, some significant differences between Sunni and Shi'ite practices. The phenomenon of 'temporary marriage', *mut'a*, considered to be referred to in Qur'an 4/24, is specifically forbidden in the Sunni world, where any limit put on the length of a marriage makes a marriage contract null and void. Divorce and inheritance laws also vary.

Most striking is a different form of the *shahada* employed at some points in Shi'ite history. The phrase 'I testify that 'Ali is the *wali* ['friend'] of God' is added to the two-part Sunni witness to faith; this is, however, a fairly late addition, mention of it not being made in the earliest texts of Shi'ite law other than that of Ibn Babawayh, who condemns its usage. The sixteenth century saw arguments in favour of its employment, urged probably by the political aims of the rulers at that time, the Safavids, who instituted Shi'ism as the state religion of Iran in 1501. The argument for the basis of the statement as opposed to its ritual employment, however, is to be found quite early in Shi'ite thought, for example in al-Kulayni who argues that the belief in the *wilaya* of 'Ali is a fundamental tenet of Shi'ism, and that the belief simply in 'there is no god but God and Muhammad is the messenger of God' is not sufficient to ensure salvation; clearly, the third element of the testimony is needed in the belief of the individual, even if in this early period it was not actually part of the ritual repetition of the *shahada*.

Additionally, Ibn Babawayh reports the following tradition about Fatima bint Asad, the mother of 'Ali. Muhammad is quoted as saying that immediately after her death, 'She was asked about her Lord, and she said, "My Lord is Allah." And she was asked about her Prophet and she replied, "Muhammad." And she was asked about her Imam and *wali* and she faltered and paused. And I said to her, "Thy son, thy son." So she said, "My Imam is my son." Thereupon they [the two questioning angels who appear to everyone after death] departed from her and said, "We have no power over you".'[13] Undoubtedly, it was the pressure of Sunni condemnation which did not allow this statement to enter the Shi'ite *shahada* from the very beginning and it was only after many centuries that it was actually approved under more propitious political circumstances.

A prominent celebration which is not found in the Sunni world revolves around the commemoration of the death of Husayn, the son of 'Ali. Culminating on the tenth day of the first month of the year, Muharram, the day of 'Ashura, it observes the day of the death of Husayn and his followers which took place at the hands of the forces of the Umayyad ruler Yazid. This occurred in the year 680. Martyrdom to the cause of the party of 'Ali became the operative motif in understanding Husayn's death and the celebration of this became the central event of the Shi'ite religious calendar. Visitation of sacred places, especially the tomb of Husayn in Karbala, plays an important role in the celebrations on this day.[14]

Variants of Shi'ism

With the notion of an Imam to be identified in each generation it is not surprising, given human nature it might even be thought, that rival claimants would appear at various points in history; we thus see the emergence of several branches within Shi'ism, all of which appear to have differed over the line of descent of authority. The Isma'ilis, Zaydis, and Druze are three such prominent groups. Some of these splits account for their origins in terms of differences over political strategy. The Zaydis, for example, picture their origins in armed revolt against the Umayyad rulers. They were formed as a group in support of Zayd ibn 'Ali, a grandson of Husayn ibn 'Ali, who was defeated and killed in 740. While in certain situations these small offshoots of Shi'ism have proved politically volatile, for the most part, throughout a good portion of their history, mainstream Shi'ites have been politically quiescent, looking forward to the end of time and the return of the Mahdi. This is simply the result of the occultation of the Imam when faced with the political realities of the historical situation.

CHAPTER NINE

Sufism

Sources of Sufism

The question of the origins of Sufism (*tasawwuf*), the mystical aspect within Islam, and its devotees, the Sufis, seems to have attracted its own particular type of dispute within the academic study of Islam. The reason for this dispute would appear to go back once again to a memory of medieval (and later) polemic between Christians and Muslims. Christians have often pictured Islam as a very sensually-based religion: Muhammad's multiple marriages, the Qur'an's very physical and sensual portrayal of heaven and its rewards, and Islam's permitting of polygamy and enjoining holy war (*jihad*) have all been featured in these kinds of characterizations. At the same time, however, Christians have been very well aware of a profound ascetic-mystical trend in Islam. Abu Hamid al-Ghazzali (d. 1111), for example, one of the most famous of all Sufis, became well known in the medieval West especially in his philosophical guise; this was true of a variety of other mystically-inspired writers as well. In trying to reconcile the two natures perceived within Islam, the implicit suggestion given by some early writers on the subject was that the mystical trend could not be inherent in Islam but must have come from Christianity, in their view a far more elevated religion.

It is the case, then, that raising the question of the origins of Sufism today is no less controversial than the question of the origins of the entire religion of Islam, because behind the questions lies the aura, if not the attitude, of medieval polemic. To suggest that Islamic mysticism is, in fact, a borrowing from outside raises the spectre of a denial of the intrinsically spiritual nature of Islam and thence of the spiritual nature of Muslims themselves.

The question of origins here is two-fold. The basic point, much argued by Sufis themselves in their search for legitimation of their spiritual quest, is whether Islam as a religion contained within it a spiritual–ascetic tendency from the very beginning; that is, does Islam inherently see the mystical way (defined, for the time being, as the quest for some intimacy with God as induced through certain practices of a meditative, repetitive, or self-denying nature) as the ideal life that should be aimed for? From the Islamic perspective, is that lifestyle inherently pleasing to God?

The second issue is one concerning the origins of Sufism itself. Regardless of where the original spiritual–ascetic impulse came from, were the practices, aspirations and the mode of expression used by the Sufis elements developed within Islam or were they the result of influence from another source (Christian, Indian, Iranian, or whatever) and adapted to an Islamic style?

The source of Sufism in Islam

The problem with answering the first question is, of course, one of interpretation. How do we judge an issue such as 'inherent asceticism'? Some would say that a basic world-denying attitude is a part of Judaism, Christianity, and Islam, especially because the over all tradition has been influenced by the radical dualism of Manichaeism with its distrust of the material world. This attitude is difficult to reconcile, however, with the picture of Islam and Judaism especially as nomocratic, where a very practical attitude towards life in the here and now, as manifested in the law, is a prime characteristic of the religion. The other aspect of the problem is the common one found in all elements of the origins of Islam: the lack of contemporary sources. There simply are no ascertainably early sources which give us a glimpse of a spiritual–ascetic lifestyle from before the ninth century.

Muslim arguments on the subject revolve around the citation of the Qur'an and elements of the *hadith* and the *sira*, the life story of Muhammad, which indicate the possibility of, if not the positive encouragement and enactment of, the ascetic ideal. This approach fully answers the question from the internal Muslim perspective. The Qur'an and Muhammad, as Sufis have always said, support the mystical quest.

Statements concerning God are popularly cited, for example, Qur'an 2/186: *Whenever My servants ask you about Me . . . I am near*, and Qur'an 50/15: *We {God} are Closer to him {humanity} than his jugular vein!*; looking inward therefore becomes the goal and the quest, although Qur'an 2/115, *wherever you may turn, there will be God's countenance*, adds another dimension to the quest. The wandering way of life of the early ascetic is supported in Qur'an 29/20, *Travel around the earth and see how He began with creation*. Qur'an 9/123 asserts *God stands by the heedful* whose way of life is echoed in the Qur'anic refrain to remember God always (for example Qur'an 33/41, *You who believe, remember God often*). The 'light verse', Qur'an 24/35, is the most famous of all verses for Sufi speculation and its very presence in the Qur'an is often claimed to be proof of the need for the mystic way: *God is the Light of Heaven and Earth! His light may be compared to a niche in which there is a lamp; the lamp is in a glass; the glass is just as if it were a glittering star kindled from a blessed olive tree, {which is} neither Eastern nor Western, whose oil will almost glow though the fire has never touched it. Light upon light, God guides anyone He wishes to His light.*[1]

As for Muhammad, his whole experience of revelation and his preparation towards receiving it are seen as models for the ascetic life and its product. This is also true of other Qur'anic figures, most especially Moses and al-Khidr whose stories, as told in *sura* 18, have been elaborated into accounts of the mystic quest. Many of the traditions about Muhammad most favoured by the Sufis are not to be found in the major *hadith* collections, generally having been rejected by the collectors as unsound, but the Sufis kept their traditions going among their own circles. Many aphorisms are found on Muhammad's lips which are applicable to the Sufi quest, and Muhammad is also portrayed as following an ascetic way of life. The latter traditions found their way into works such as the *Kitab al-Zuhd* of Ibn Hanbal (d. 855), the eponym of the legal school, who is often seen as a supporter of the early ascetic movement.[2] Poverty especially became an ideal espoused by Muhammad.

Even more productive for the Sufis has been the story of the *mi'raj*, Muhammad's night journey (based around Qur'an 17/1), which is seen as a tale of the supreme mystical experience to which every mystic aspires. While the basic account is found in all orthodox sources about Muhammad, starting in germ form in Muhammad's early biographer Ibn Ishaq, the Sufi understanding and interpretation of the account are, of course, unique. The emphasis frequently falls on the role of the journey as a prophetic initiation, leading the way for all mystics after Muhammad to journey to their own union with the divine presence, not as prophets but as saints or 'friends of God'.

Interestingly, there is a marked anti-ascetic tendency within the Sunni books of *hadith*, especially focusing on the rejection of Christian monasticism. For example, these reports are often used in Islam to support the notion that even Sufis should marry. Other such elements include a rejection of forty-day food restrictions and pleas against poverty (even to the point of denying excessive charity).[3] Most of this material can be seen as anti-Christian in tendency and as reflecting the tension Muslims felt over the status of ascetic tendencies in early Islam.

However, all of this attention to the Qur'an, *sira*, and *hadith* on the part of the Sufis simply indicates that they have, like all other Muslims, always gone back to the prime sources of Islam for inspiration as well as justification of their position; in that way they are no different from the jurists in the quest to define the law as closely as possible, for example. For modern historians to take 'objective' facts from this type of material and attempt to reconstruct a picture of mystical trends in early Islam is to commit the error of anachronistic reading of texts; one is clearly looking at the texts through the eyes of later people and we learn nothing from them of the earliest meaning given to these sources. The most that may be concluded from this part of the discussion, therefore, is simply to say that Muslims have found the life story of Muhammad and the Qur'an itself to be vital sources in their mystical quest. One would not want to discount the possibility that even the early versions of the biography (*sira*) of Muhammad have been affected by early mystics and thus reflect some of their concerns and desires, as is reflected also in the *hadith* literature with its books devoted to *zuhd*, asceticism, as practiced by Muhammad. That the Qur'an might in fact contain such ascetic elements is a possibility that needs to be entertained; however, whether the pieces of the Qur'an which suggest this background were always understood that way by Muslims, and where those pieces of the Qur'an actually originated, are vexing questions which still must be faced by scholars.

Sources of Sufi practice

The solution to this first aspect of the problem of the origins of Sufism, then, would seem to be to put aside the questions concerning the inherent spiritual asceticism of Islam and perhaps simply admit that the understanding of the nature of God as contained within the Judeo-Christian-Muslim tradition is one which is potentially amenable to the mystical way of life. There only remains, then, the second question of the development of what we may truly call Sufism in Islam, the influences upon it and its role in the emergence of Islam. For the early period there is the major problem of definition, of how to determine for example, whether Ibn Hanbal should be considered a Sufi or simply an ascetic Muslim, given his encouragement of that way of life. That he should have combined this role with one of the upholding of traditionalism is significant, of course; one of his works which displays ascetic tendencies is the above-mentioned *Kitab al-zuhd*, a collection of traditions about the life of Muhammad. Indeed, for the earliest period, this emphasis on asceticism is the primary element that one can isolate with certainty as the forerunner of the later mystical way. The evidence suggests that it was in the early to mid-ninth century that these sorts of tendencies found their expression in written form; it was only later in that century that this became combined with speculative thought, producing as a result a true system of mysticism which may accurately and meaningfully be called Sufism. The dating of this era for the emergence of Sufism is confirmed within juridical works, where disdain for the ascetic way of life is displayed and a resultant attempt on the part of the jurists to restrict its scope can clearly be seen; the end of the eighth and the early ninth century appears to have been the era of the greatest disputes on this matter.[4]

Certainly the influence of Christianity on the foundation of asceticism in Islam is clear in some of the earliest writings. Al-Muhasibi (d. 837), for example, has been shown[5] to have borrowed heavily from the New Testament for various sayings and commendations of the Sufi way of life. Also, the practice of wearing woollen garments called *suf*, from which it is popularly believed that the term 'Sufi' (meaning 'those who wear rough woollen garments') was coined, is said to have been done in imitation of Christian hermits; this was in order to serve as an indication of poverty as well as being an ascetic practice in and by itself.

The development of a mystical litany was also a part of the early enunciation of the movement. Termed *dhikr*, the practice was connected by the Sufis to the Qur'anic injunction to 'mention God often' as in Qur'an 33/21. The developed form of this litany consists of the constant repetition of various phrases, often *la-ilah illa Allah*, 'there is no god but God'. This practice serves as the focal point of devotions for virtually every Sufi group.[6] Christian modes of worship once again may have provided some of the impetus for this particular element.

Doctrinally, the early mystics are held to have been devoted to the notion of *tawakkul*, total trust in God. The characteristics are complete indifference to the world and its affairs and a full dependence upon God supplying the needs of the individual; this attitude was said to demonstrate one's total trust in the power and mercy of God who will supply those needs, it was believed. A total lack of possessions and deprivation of any bodily comforts was the mark of such a person. This trend is often seen to have been influenced by Christianity also, being a tendency of monasticism in the church.

Given the geographical contexts in which Islamic asceticism is generally seen to have emerged – Baghdad, in the environment of the Christian heritage and Khurasan, a former Buddhist centre – it is not surprising that elements of various religions (especially Christianity as the above examples show) should be present and little would seem to be gained by denying it. However, it has frequently been pointed out that the ascetic lifestyle in Islam developed with a certain overt political motivation: once again in Islam, a religious position appears to have been used as a rallying point for rebellion against the ruling powers. The whole early ascetic inclination is frequently pictured as a renunciation and rejection of the political strife in the formative Islamic period. The early mystics were the true Muslims who held onto the Islamic spirit in face of the manipulation of the religion by the ruling powers for their own purposes. The emphasis on *tawakkul* would be pictured in marked contrast to the efforts of all other Muslims to secure their places on earth rather than in heaven, at least from the perspective of the mystics. Al-Hasan al-Basri (d. 728), famous for his role in the theological debates discussed in chapter 5, above, emerges in the literature as one of the central figures of this type of spirituality, going to the extent of denying the value of existence in this world and speaking of the hereafter as the realm free of the contamination of political self-interest. Revolutionary involvement in the political arena was not sanctioned by al-Hasan al-Basri, even if that could have meant replacing an unjust ruler by a pious one; the slow persuasion of rulers was the best that could be hoped for in the effort to improve the lot of all Muslims in the community.

Over all, then, the argument certainly can be made for 'foreign influences' on the development of Sufism but, without a doubt, modern scholarship sees the internal tensions of the Muslim community as crucial to the emergence of early ascetic tendencies.

Development of Sufism

The ninth century was marked by a rapid progression of mystics, each famous for adding a certain element to the emergent mystical viewpoint and creating the central tenets of Sufism. Under the influence of neo-Platonism, at least according to some writers, mystical doctrines of the love of God, the beatific vision of the mystical experience, gnosis as the goal of the experience, the image of the mystical ascension, the absorption into God, and the theory of the mystical states are all seen to emerge.

Al-Junayd

Al-Junayd (d. 910), a pupil of al-Muhasibi, is often given the credit for establishing a true system of mystical speculation, bringing together the insights of his predecessors and creating a lasting system for all subsequent generations. He is credited with the elaboration of the doctrine of *fana'*, the goal of the mystic in 'dying in one's self', 'passing away', or 'absorption' into God, supported by the Qur'anic *Everyone upon it {the earth} will disappear while your Lord's face remains full of majesty and splendour* (Qur'an 55/26). The mystic quest is based on the need to return to God, the state in which humanity was before creation. *Baqa'*, the 'continuance', is the existence of the mystic after *fana'*, when he or she lives in God. Al-Junayd combined this goal with an ethical theory which demanded of the mystic who has reached the state of 'absorption' a return to society; this was so that the individual would make clear 'the evidence of [God's] grace to him, so that the lights of His gifts in the return of his individual characteristics scintillate and attract the community to him who appreciate him.'[7] This meant, for al-Junayd, that the Sufi had the responsibility to return to his community life and fulfil all the obligations of Muslim existence; the knowledge of the individual's absorption into the divine remains a 'secret treasure' which shines through the person in everything done in the world.

Al-Hallaj

Contemporary with al-Junayd was al-Hallaj (d. 922) who likewise was convinced of the necessity of the mystic quest but who was condemned to death for the blasphemy of considering that individuals could recognize their God-nature through mystical experience. Stories relate that al-Hallaj proclaimed 'I am the Truth' which was taken to mean that he felt himself actually to be God incarnate in the world. Such Sufis (another early example is al-Bistami, d. 875) have come to be termed 'intoxicated' as compared to the 'sober' mysticism of al-Junayd, for they had become so overcome by the mystical experience that existence as such had no meaning to them; their utterances became the focal point of their understanding of their experiences and vice-versa.[8] The ethical aspect of al-Junayd's doctrine became submerged within their experiences.

Al-Sarraj

These authors were only starting to develop a truly systematic picture of Sufism; it fell to authors such as Abu Nasr al-Sarraj (d. 988) in the following century to construct general accounts of Sufism, its history and its meaning in the Islamic context. Al-Sarraj wrote in his *Kitab al-luma'* of the legitimacy of Sufi practice, based upon the precedent of Muhammad and his companions. With this he combined a great deal of definitional material in an attempt to distill the essence of the mystical path as it existed in his time. He states, for example,

> The meaning of 'passing away' and 'continuance' . . . is the passing away of ignorance into the abiding condition of knowledge and the passing away of disobedience into the abiding state of obedience, and the passing away of indifference into the state of continual worship, and the passing away of the consideration of the actions of the servant, which are temporary, into the vision of the Divine Grace, which is the eternal.[9]

Al-Qushayri

The eleventh century brought greater systematization to the theoretical basis of Sufism in the writings of al-Qushayri (d. 1072). Writing in 1046, al-Qushayri was concerned with demonstrating that Sufism was not in conflict with Sunni Islam. Part of this proof was provided by the biography of many prominent Sufis. He also presented a picture of the theory of the stations through which a Sufi passes on his or her mystic quest and the states which God may grace the mystic with during that quest. Such had already been detailed by al-Sarraj before him, but al-Qushayri added further detail to the schema. Forty-five terms are used to describe the quest, starting with *tawba*, 'repentance', which is seen as the manifestation of the conscious desire to follow the mystic way, through 'patience', 'constant awareness of God' and 'satisfaction with God' culminating in 'gnosis', 'love' and 'yearning to be with God'.[10]

Al-Ghazzali

Abu Hamid al-Ghazzali used the basis established by earlier Sufi theorists for promoting the assimilation of Sufism into orthodoxy in developing his own arguments; his magnum opus, *Ihya' 'ulum al-din*, the 'Revivification of the Religious Sciences' written between 1099 and 1102, tried to accomplish just what its title suggests: to bring life back into the orthodox 'religious sciences' through the inspiration of Sufism. In the process, Sufism itself would be seen to gain total legitimacy as being an essential part of the Islamic way of life. His work is divided into four sections. The first, worship, concentrates on the 'inner meaning' of the rituals of Islam. The second, personal behaviour, sees the progression from religious law to mystical training as intimately linked. The third, deadly sins, details the discipline needed for the mystic quest. Finally the fourth, the way to salvation, concentrates on the interpretation of spiritual experience. This progress in the life of the individual reflects al-Ghazzali's over all view of life and the mystic quest:

> If, then, you ask, 'What is the Beginning of Guidance in order that I may test my soul thereby?' know that the beginning of guidance is outward piety and the end of guidance is inward piety. Only through piety is anything really achieved; only the pious are guided. Piety designates carrying out the commands of God most high and turning aside from what He prohibits.[11]

The Sufi orders

The tendency towards increased intellectual support and systematization of Sufism was developed even further in the Sufi orders which are based on the principle of the relationship between the master and the pupil; the authority of the master who has ascended through the stages of the mystic must be accepted wholly by the pupil, for only with guidance will the union with God be possible. The foundation of the *tariqa*, the 'way' or 'path', and later coming to mean the 'order' or 'brotherhood', emerged as a way of providing a practical and structured way for the initiate to be guided through the stages of mystical experience; beginning as an informal group, companionship with an acknowledged master was the focal point of the *tariqa*. Groups emerged early on, centred in dwellings known as *ribat*s, *khanaqah*s, *khalwa*s or *zawiya*s, all meaning 'Sufi retreats' in one part or another of the Muslim world. Such retreats were not organized in any particular way, however; the participants simply wandered from one such place to another. In the eleventh century the institutionalized *tariqa* movement received a boost with the Seljuq reorganization of the *madrasa*, the Islamic school, and their support and supervision of Sufi dwellings at the same time. This trend was encouraged even further by the success of al-Ghazzali's work in bringing Sufism into the folds of orthodoxy. The process culminated in the thirteenth century with the emergence of special centres of Sufi training; focused on the activities and way of a single man, a centre would perpetuate the name, teaching, exercises, and rule of life of that person. The *tariqa* was handed down through the *isnad* or *silsila* of the *shaykh*, the leader of the order, passing on to the spiritual heirs of that person. The initiate swore allegiance to the *shaykh*, and thereby became linked to the spiritual chain. Often incorporated into these *silsila*s were famous Sufis of the past, such as al-Junayd and al-Bistami; the initial stage of the chain is always Muhammad and from him 'Ali, although this does not necessarily indicate any Shi'ite leanings on the part of the groups.

All such *tariqa*s, formally at the very least, accept the law and ritual of orthodox Islam as binding. In this way, they provide a supplement to the Islamic way of life, rather than a true 'alternative vision', although obviously, their view of the true nature of Islam and its purpose is different from those who remain outside the *tariqa*. The point remained, however, that in order for the *tariqa*s to ensure their acceptance by orthodoxy (i.e. the jurists), the attention to the externals of Islamic life continued to be necessary.

The major *tariqa*s in classical Islam were the Suhrawardiyya, the Qadiriyya, the Rifa'iyya, the Yasawiyya, the Kubrawiyya, the Cishtiyya, the Shadhiliyya, the Badawiyya, the Mawlawiyya, and the Naqshabandiyya.[12] These groups trace their foundations to various persons who lived in the twelfth and thirteenth centuries.

The practices of the Sufi orders

Taking the Qadiriyya as an example of the *tariqa* phenomenon, one may see the role these institutions played in the fostering of the Sufi attitude. 'Abd al-Qadir al-Jilani, the *shaykh* of the movement was born in Jilan in Persia in 1077 and went to Baghdad at the age of 18; there he became a popular preacher within the Hanbali tradition at the age of about 50, and he died in 1116. There is no evidence that he ever consciously set out to form a Sufi school, although the legends told in great profusion about his life certainly want to picture him as a Sufi miracle worker.

A certain Isma'il relates the following. In front of my farmhouse there stood two date palms which had been dead for years. One day, 'Abd al-Qadir passed by on his way to see 'Ali ibn Hayti, one of his disciples who was ill. He asked me for water to perform his ablutions; he then completed a prayer of two *rak'a*s, followed by meditation. I offered him food but he said that he was not hungry. All he took was some milk. When he left, the dead trees began to sprout leaves and blossoms, and that season we had fresh dates for weeks. The grain harvest was double the normal size and there were twice as many calves in my herd as in other years. In the years after that event, this blessing continued to accompany my work, ever since 'Abd al-Qadir's visit.[13]

It was to the two sons of 'Abd al-Qadir that the formation of the school actually fell and, by the year 1300, centres existed in Iraq and Syria, with the major expansion coming in the fifteenth century. 'Abd al-Qadir himself is famed as a saint and the belief in his power of intercession has made the *tariqa* a significant presence throughout the Islamic world.

The Qadiriyya's practices reflect the beliefs of the group itself but also the general Sufi stance on the role of the master and the efficacy of various mystical practices. Their initiation procedure contains the promise to 'recite the *dhikr* in obedience to the dictates of the *shaykh*' and the *shaykh* accepts the initiate 'as a son'. The *dhikr* itself is recited by the group seated in front of the *shaykh* and can be repeated hundreds of times. The novice members repeat *la-ilah illa Allah*, 'there is no god but God', 165 times, while the more advanced members repeat a series of statements praising God and 'Abd al-Qadir 121 times, followed by 100 repetitions of *sura* 36, 41 repetitions of *sura* 72, 121 repetitions of *sura* 110, 8 repetitions of *sura* 1, topped off by one recitation of *sura* 112[15]. All this is done under the control of the *shaykh* at a pace which increases as it goes on, until individual members may, potentially have a mystic experience appropriate to the level of their spiritual advancement.

Ibn 'Arabi

Muhyi'l-Din ibn 'Arabi represents the culmination of another strand within Islamic Sufism. Born in Spain in 1165, he travelled throughout North Africa and the Middle East, becoming initiated into Sufism in 1194, and eventually dying in Damascus in 1240. He was a prolific author and wrote *al-Futuhat al-Makkiyya*, 'The Meccan revelations', a Sufi encyclopedia, and *Fusus al-hikam*, 'The Bezels of Wisdom', his most famous work which summarizes his vision. A difficult writer to comprehend, he was fully educated in the Islamic sciences and brought to his work a vast quantity of learning.

His thought represents a true theosophy, believing in the essential unity between humanity and God. Having brought speculative Sufism to its apogee through his emphasis on gnosis (*ma'rifa*) as the way to the experience of truth, Ibn 'Arabi has been accused of monism: of denying the reality of the separation between God and His creation. The doctrine of God's transcendence is often held to be essential to Muslim orthodox theology, denying as it does any possibility of the incarnation of God in the world, a consequence of its ancient polemic with Christianity. In theory, the theosophical Sufis got around the problem with the notion of 'the reality of Muhammad' in control of the universe, that being the power to which the Sufis could aspire in their mystical quest. Ibn 'Arabi argued for the doctrine of *wahdat al-wujud*, the 'unity of being', where certain implications seem hard to avoid: being and existence are all one and are combined in God; being which is apart from God exists only by virtue of His will, but was, prior to its being made separate, one with God; the 'perfect human' (*al-insan al-kamil*) is the one who knows of oneness with God, who loves God and who is loved by God.

The role of Sufism

The influence of Ibn 'Arabi, despite the complexity of his thought, has been enormous, not only on all Sufism from that point on but also in the modern scholarly world which is still trying to come to grips with his ideas.[16] But Sufism was not only of this elevated intellectual type, for the role of the brotherhoods in bringing Sufism closer to the popular level cannot be underestimated. It was the efforts of the brotherhoods which spread Islam into many far-flung corners of the contemporary Muslim world, often facilitated by means of mystical poetry and aided by a tolerant attitude towards local religious practices as long as they were accompanied by the basic spiritual impulse of Islam in its Sufi guise. Sufism has also served throughout its history as a source of religious revival for Muslims, breathing life into institutions when they tended to reach the point of self-suffocation. While many of the orthodox have remained deeply suspicious of many Sufi practices and at certain points in history (most notably with Ibn Taimiyya, d. 1328) renewal of Islam has been sought by means of a purge of Sufi influences, Sufism has remained alive and well, catering to those who picture life in terms of the 'mystic quest.'

CHAPTER TEN

Conclusion: the literary formation of Islam

It is possible to see the development of tradition as a dynamic matching of the literary tradition with the needs and capacities of later readers. [1]

In order to study the formative period of Islam, the main evidence we have before us is found embodied in the Muslim literary tradition. This is a tradition which has been creatively formed and read by Muslims throughout their history. This reading and re-reading is not a process which has come to an end; indeed, the vitality of Islam – of religion in general – may be seen in the way in which it brings forward the past and reforms it – re-reads it – in ways appropriate to the contemporary situation.

For the modern student of religion, this creates something of a dilemma: how to get back within this re-reading process of the sources and understand the formative influences that brought the subject of study into being. It may be, in fact, that we can never fully enter into this process, standing as do we within creative re-readings of our own culture and time. But we can come to some understanding of the fluctuations of these re-readings and people's responses to them and that is what this book has tried to do with the Islamic sources.

In the emergence of Islam as a religion, there seem to be two major factors displayed in the sources which can be isolated and examined. One relates to the formation of Islam as a distinct entity alongside Judaism and Christianity. The other relates to social issues and the matter of authority in the community.

The emergence of the identity of Islam appears to have been a dynamic process, working on many levels at the same time. Also the idea of the 'distinct' Islam appears to have existed in tension with a tendency to picture Islam as the continuation of Judaism and Christianity. The Dome of the Rock provides a graphic illustration of this point both in its physical structure and in its inscriptional ('textual') contents. Built on a site significant to Judaism and in a style significant to Christianity, the building represents a continuation of both of those traditions, an embracing of the sacred tradition of the pre-Islamic dispensations. Yet, at the same time, it stands for a disavowal of those traditions. The rejection of the central theological tenets of Christianity and the assertion of the identity of the new religion Islam is reflected in the inscriptions inside the building; this is to be combined with an interpretation of the political emblem presented by the actual physical construction of the Dome, which acts as a reinforcement of the sense of Islam's dissociation from its forerunners.

Likewise, in a theological vein, Muslims reacted to arguments with Jews and especially Christians, and this has found its manifestations in texts; that is, written polemical argumentation appears to have been a major formative element in creating an identity of Islam seen to be both separate from the other two religions and, at the same time, intimately connected with them. The rejection of the scriptural texts and various central tenets held by Judaism and Christianity allowed Islam to form its own identity; however, the areas in which Islam did assert its own identity in theological terms are those which were dictated by the agenda found in the polemical arguments. Thus the emphasis fell on discussions of God's attributes and of free will.

The second factor which emerges from the examination of the literary tradition reveals that one of the major questions throughout the formative period of Islam was who embodies authority and how that authority is to be exercised within the community. A basic struggle took place between those in political power and those who emerged as a class of scholarly elite resisting the assertions of caliphal power. In the earliest times, when Islam was forming, a unified community under the leadership of the caliph appears to have existed. A rival power base emerged, however, both as a result of intellectual reflection on Islam (and the emergence of a concept of ultimate authority residing in God alone) and as a result of politico-religious objections to the existing power structure. The creation of the two main groups of Muslims, Sunnis and Shi'ites, was the result of discussions and arguments over authority. Within the grouping which became the Sunnis, the scholars were able to wrest control away from the caliph as a consequence of politically unwise (in retrospect) stratagems on the part of the caliph, manifested in the institution of the *mihna*. The scholars asserted their own authority as textually based by upholding the Qur'an and *sunna*. The other response to the situation, which resulted in the Shi'ites, was a continuation of a centralized authority, but vested in the figure of the Imam. Eventually, however, even that became inconvenient for the pretensions of the emerging scholarly class, and the removal of the Imam into 'occultation' ultimately produced a society whose structures of authority, on a practical level, differed very little from the Sunni version.

At the base of all these discussions – whether over identity or authority – are the Qur'an and the *hadith*, linked to God and the person of Muhammad. These, too, are texts: texts which are in themselves creative re-readings of the past. But they are texts which have gained central symbolic authority within the Muslim community by being connected to both divine revelation and divine protection. In that respect as well though, these sources are following the tradition of that past of which they are re-readings, the tradition of the earlier religious dispensations of the Near East. Thereby the basis for the establishment of a new tradition called Islam was created for those who wished to embrace that identity, understanding of authority, and relationship to God.

Glossary

'Abbasids	dynasty of caliphs ruling from 750, through the era of the flowering of Islam, and coming to a final end in 1258, although they had lost any meaningful power several centuries earlier with the rise of the Buwayhids.
Allah	Arabic for God.
Ash'arites	followers of the theological school named after al-Ash'ari (d. 935).
aya	verse of the Qur'an.
basmala	the statement at the beginning of each *sura* of the Qur'an (except *sura* 9), 'In the name of God, the Mercy-giving, the Merciful!' (frequently also translated 'In the name of God, the Merciful, the Compassionate'), also used by Muslims as an invocation.
Buwayhids	dynasty of Shi'ite Persian military rulers, taking over in 945 and lasting until the takeover of the Sunni Seljuq rulers in 1055.
dhikr	'mentioning' or 'remembrance'; term used for the chant in Sufi meditations.
fiqh	jurisprudence, the science of religious law, as described by the jurists, the *fuqaha'*.
ghayba	'occultation' of the last Imam in the Shi'ite tradition.

hadith   a tradition or written report, being the source material for the *sunna* of Muhammad.

hajj   pilgrimage to Mecca done in the month of Dhu'l-hijja, one of the 'Five Pillars' of Islam.

Hanbalites   followers of the Sunni school of law named after Ahmad ibn Hanbal (d. 855).

hanif   the attribute, especially ascribed to Abraham in the Qur'an, of being a sincere believer in God.

Hanifites   followers of the Sunni school of law named after Abu Hanifa (d. 767).

Hijaz   region in the west of central Arabia, the birthplace of Muhammad.

hijra   Muhammad's emigration from Mecca to Medina, understood as the date for the beginning of the *hirji* calendar.

i'jaz   doctrine which states that the Qur'an cannot be imitated; the 'inimitability' of the Qur'an.

ijma'   'consensus', one of the sources of law.

imam   (1) the prayer leader in the *salat*; (2) when capitalized in this book as Imam, one of the revered early leaders of the Shi'ites, the source of authority in that community, being 'Ali ibn abi Talib and certain of his descendants who inherited the position.

Imami   generic name given to the largest group of Shi'ites, the Ithna 'Ashariyya.

iman   faith.

isma'   doctrine which states that the prophets, and most especially Muhammad, were protected from sin (*ma'sum*) during their lifetimes (also applied to Shi'ite Imams).

isnad   chain of authorities through whom a *hadith* report has passed, the statement of which comprises the first part of the *hadith* report, the text being the *matn*.

isra'   Muhammad's 'night journey' to Jerusalem.

jahiliyya   'Age of Ignorance', historically seen to be before Muhammad but referring religiously to ignoring, or ignorance of, Islam.

jihad   'striving for the faith' or 'holy war', sometimes seen as a 'sixth pillar' of Islam.

jinn   'sprites' or genies, another dimension to the creation on earth.

Ka'ba	the sacred black cube building in the middle of the mosque in Mecca, towards which Muslims pray.
kalam	literally, 'speech'; refers to a mode of theological discussion framed in terms of an argument and thence to speculative theology as a whole.
khalifa	Caliph, the leader of the Sunni community, the 'successor' to Muhammad.
Kharijites	group in early Islam who believed in absolute devotion as the mark of a true Muslim, all others being unbelievers.
madhhab	school of law.
Malikites	followers of the legal school named after Malik ibn Anas (d. 795).
matn	the text of a *hadith* report.
Maturidites	followers of the theological school named after al-Maturidi (d. 944).
mi'raj	the 'heavenly ascension' of Muhammad.
Murji'a	group in early Islam who held the 'status quo' position in the debates over faith, generally connected to Abu Hanifa (d. 767).
Mu'tazila	developers of a school of thought stressing human free will and the unity and justice of God who embraced Greek rationalism.
Qadariyya	group in early Islam who argued for free will in the theological debates, precursors of the Mu'tazila.
qadi	judge who makes decisions on the basis of the religious law.
qibla	the direction in which one faces in prayer (Mecca), marked by the *mihrab* in the mosque.
qiyas	'analogy', one of the sources of law in Sunni Islam.
salat	the prescribed five prayers a day, one of the 'Five Pillars'.
sawm	fasting performed in the month of Ramadan, one of the 'Five Pillars'.
Shafi'ites	followers of the school of law named after al-Shafi'i (d. 820).
shahada	'witness to faith', saying (in Arabic) 'There is no god but God and Muhammad is His messenger', one of the 'Five Pillars'.
shari'a	the religious law derived from the Qur'an and the *sunna*.

Glossary

shaykh	literally, 'an old man' and used as a term of respect for a religious teacher; used especially of a Sufi master.
Shi'ites	the religio-political party championing the claims of 'Ali and his heirs to the rightful leadership of the community and to their status as Imams.
sira	the biography of Muhammad.
Sufi	an adherent to the mystical way.
sunna	'custom'; the way Muhammad acted which is then emulated by Muslims.
Sunnis	the majority form of Islam, those who follow the *sunna* (the *ahl al-sunna*), who do not recognize the authority of the Shi'ite Imams.
sura	a chapter of the Qur'an.
tariqa	'the way' of Sufism; a Sufi order or brotherhood.
tasawwuf	Sufism, the mystical way in Islam.
tawhid	doctrine of the unity of God.
Traditionalists	term used primarily for the followers of Ibn Hanbal (d. 855) who rejected the claims of rationalism especially in early theological discussions.
'ulama'	the learned class, especially those learned in religious matters.
Umayyads	the first dynasty of caliphs, ruling from 661 until the takeover of the 'Abbasids in 750.
'umra	the 'visitation' of the holy places in Mecca, the lesser pilgrimage.
wilaya	position of 'Ali as the 'friend' (*wali*) of God.
zakat	alms tax, one of the 'Five Pillars'.

Notes

Preface and introductory material

1　Hans Mol, *Identity and the Sacred: a Sketch for a New Social-Scientific Theory of Religion*, New York, The Free Press, 1976, p. 55.

2　Unfortunately, the various editions of the *Encyclopaedia of Islam* are not consistent in their transliteration. The older edition, for example, uses 'ai' for the diphthong 'ay'. The transliteration of the new edition has been followed here in every case, with the exceptions noted.

Chapter 1　Pre-history

1　A brief and useful summary of the history of this period with excellent attention to the religious factors involved is to be found in F. E. Peters, *Allah's Commonwealth. A History of Islam in the Near East 600–1100 A.D.*, New York, Simon & Schuster, 1973, introduction.

2　See J. Spencer Trimingham, *Christianity among the Arabs in pre-Islamic Times*, London, Longman, 1979, chapter 5.

3　On the matter of the role of trade in South Arabia and its bearing on the rise of Islam see Patricia Crone, *Meccan Trade and the Rise of Islam*, Princeton, NJ, Princeton University Press, 1987, pp. 12ff, 27.

4　On this aspect of South Arabian religion, see Ulf Oldenburg 'Above the stars of El. El in ancient South Arabian religion', *Zeitschrift für die alttestamentliche Wissenschaft*, 82 (1970), 187–208.

5　See G. Ryckmans, 'Heaven and earth in the South Arabian inscriptions', *Journal of Semitic Studies*, 3 (1958), 225–36.

6 See Crone, op. cit.

7 See Joseph Henninger, 'Pre-islamic bedouin religion', in Merlin L. Swartz (trans. and ed.) *Studies on Islam*, New York, Oxford University Press, 1981, pp. 3–22, although much of the detail in this article is open to grave doubt.

8 See G. R. Hawting, 'The origins of Muslim Santuary at Mecca', in G. H. A. Juynboll (ed.) *Studies in the first Century of Islamic Society*, Carbondale, IL, Southern Illinois University Press, 1982, pp. 23–47.

9 See Edward Shils, 'Tradition', *Comparative Studies in Society and History*, 13 (1971), 122–59.

10 See e.g. al-Wahidi, *Kitab asbab al-nuzul* (Ahmad Saqr, ed.), Cairo, Dar al-kitab al-Jadid, 1969, pp. 43–4. On the interpretation of this type of anecdote, see A. Rippin, 'The exegetical function of *asbab al-nuzul* material', *Bulletin of the School of Oriental and African Studies*, 51 (1988), 1–20.

11 Compare Qur'an 5/103.

12 See, for example, Michael Cook, *Muhammad*, Oxford University Press, 1983, chapter 7.

13 Al-Wahidi, op. cit., p. 42.

14 See al-Wahidi, op. cit., pp. 41–2. On this passage and its interpretation, see Mahmoud M. Ayoub, *The Qur'an and its Interpreters*, vol. 1, Albany, NY, State University of New York Press, 1984, pp. 176–9.

15 See Michael Cook, 'Early Islamic dietary law', *Jerusalem Studies in Arabic and Islam*, 7 (1986), 217–77, especially pp. 270–1.

16 Ibn al-Kalbi, *Kitab al-asnam* (R. Klinke-Rosenberger, ed.), Leipzig, Otto Harrassowitz, 1941, pp. 3–4; a full English translation of this work is available, Nabih Amin Faris, *The Book of Idols, being a Translation from the Arabic of the Kitab al-Asnam by Hisham ibn al-Kalbi*, Princeton, NJ, Princeton University Press, 1952.

Chapter 2   The Qur'an

1 See *Encyclopaedia of Islam*, 'mala'ika'.

2 See Andrew Rippin and Jan Knappert (eds), *Textual Sources for the Study of Islam*, Manchester, Manchester University Press, 1987, section 2.1.7.

3 See Arthur Jeffery, 'The Qur'an as scripture', *The Muslim World*, 40 (1950), especially pp. 202–6.

4 See John Burton, *The Collection of the Qur'an*, Cambridge, Cambridge University Press, 1977, for a treatment of these various accounts and their potential significance.

5 See John Wansbrough, *Quranic Studies: Sources and Methods of Scriptural Interpretation*, Oxford, Oxford University Press, 1977, section 4.

6 William Muir, *The Apology of al-Kindy, written at the Court of al-Mamun (A.H. 215; A.D. 830) in Defence of Christianity against Islam*, London, Smith, Elder & Co., 1882, pp. 18–19 and 28, passages slightly modified.

7   See Rippin and Knappert, op. cit., section 2.3, for a partial translation of al-Rummani's text.

8   See the ongoing translation of this work, J. Cooper, *The Commentary on the Qur'an by Abu Ja'far Muhammad b. Jarir al-Tabari*, Oxford, Oxford University Press, 1987–. For further bibliography of Qur'anic interpretation see Andrew Rippin, 'The present status of *tafsir* studies', *The Muslim World*, 72 (1982), 224–38.

9   See the passage from the *hadith* collection of Muslim ibn al-Hajjaj translated in Rippin and Knappert, op. cit., section 3.2.3.2.

10 See al-Bukhari, *al-Sahih*, *Kitab fada'il al-Qur'an*, Cairo, Dar al-'Arabi, 1955, vol. 6, pp. 103–6, in the translation of Muhammad Muhsin Khan, *Sahih al-Bukhari*, New Delhi, Kitab Bhavan, 1984 (5th edition), vol. 6, pp. 489–96. For a somewhat later treatment of the same subject see A. E. Christensen, *Xavass-i-Ayat. Notices et extraits d'un manuscrit persan traitant la magie des versets du Coran*, Copenhagen, A. F. Host & Son, 1920.

11 For interesting examples of this, see Bess Allen Donaldson, *The Wild Rue. A Study of Muhammadan Magic and Folklore in Iran*, London, Luzac, 1938, chapter 16.

Chapter 3   Muhammad

1   See Patricia Crone and Michael Cook, *Hagarism, The Making of the Islamic World*, Cambridge, Cambridge University Press, 1977; Michael Cook, *Muhammad*, Oxford, Oxford University Press, 1983.

2   For an attempt to use the Qur'an as a historical source for the life of Muhammad see A. T. Welch, 'Muhammad's understanding of himself: the Koranic data', in R. G. Hovannisian and S. Vryonis Jr. (eds), *Islam's Understanding of Itself*, Malibu, CA, Undena Publications, 1983, pp. 15–52. It must be remembered, however, that the only way the author is able to draw the conclusions which he does is by assuming, *a priori*, the basic framework provided by the *Sira* material.

3   For details of the understanding of this see Andrew Rippin, 'Al-Zarkashi and al-Suyuti on the function of the "occasion of revelation" material', *Islamic Culture*, 59 (1985), 2432–58.

4   See Lawrence I. Conrad, 'Abraha and Muhammad: some observations apropos of chronology and literary *topoi* in the early Arabic historical tradition', *Bulletin of the School of Oriental and African Studies*, 50 (1987), 225–40; on a similar tendency in historical texts also see his 'Seven and the *tasbi*': on the implications of numerical symbolism for the study of medieval Islamic history', *Journal of the Economic and Social History of the Orient*, 31 (1988), 42–73.

5   See Crone and Cook, op. cit., p. 157, n.39 and p. 160, n.56.

6   See Andrew Rippin and Jan Knappert (eds), *Textual Sources for the Study of*

Islam, Manchester, Manchester University Press, section 3.2.4.

7 Compare this standard presentation with Patricia Crone, *Meccan Trade and the Rise of Islam*, Princeton, NJ, Princeton University Press, 1987, for some insights into the historical problems of Muhammad's biography.

8 See John Wansbrough, *The Sectarian Milieu. Content and Composition of Islamic Salvation History*, Oxford, Oxford University Press, 1978, p. 32.

9 ibid., p. 56.

10 Al-Bukhari, *al-Sahih*, *Kitab fada'il al-Qur'an*, Cairo, Dar al-'Arabi, 1955, vol. 6, p. 114, in the translation of Muhammad Muhsin Khan, *Sahih al-Bukhari*, New Delhi, Kitab Bhavan, 1984 (5th edition), vol. 6, pp. 517–18, tradition number 574.

11 Al-Tirmidhi, *al Jami'*, *Kitab al-qadar*, Cairo, Dar Ihya' turath al-'Arabi, 1937–65, vol. 4, p. 445, tradition number 2135; also cited Kenneth Cragg and Marston Speight (eds), *Islam from Within: Anthology of a Religion*, Belmont, CA, Wadsworth Publishing, 1980, p. 82.

12 Classic scholarly statements of this understanding of the growth of *hadith* are to be found in Ignaz Goldziher, *Muslim Studies*, London, George Allen & Unwin, 1971, vol. 2, pp. 17–251, and Joseph Schacht, *The Origins of Muhammadan Jurisprudence*, Oxford, Clarendon Press, 1950.

13 See the works of M. J. Kister, *Studies in Jahiliya and Early Islam*, London, Variorum, 1980; also Harris Birkeland, *The Lord Guideth: Studies on Primitive Islam*, Oslo, H. Aschehoug, 1950.

14 Al-Ghazzali, *Ihya' 'ulum al-din*, as quoted in Kees Wagtendonk, 'Images in Islam, discussion of a paradox', in Dirk van der Plas (ed.), *Effigies Dei. Essays on the History of Religion*, Leiden, E. J. Brill, 1987, p. 123.

15 See Marie Rose Seguy, *The Miraculous Journey of Mahomet: Miraj Namah*, New York, George Braziller, 1977.

16 Ibn Ishaq, *al-Sira al-nabawiya*, al-Saqa, al-Abyari, Shalbi (eds), Cairo, Halabi, 1955, vol. 1, pp. 402–3; see A. Guillaume, *The Life of Muhammad. A Translation of {Ibn} Ishaq's Sirat Rasul Allah*, Oxford, Oxford University Press, 1955, p. 184.

17 See Rippin and Knappert, op. cit., section 3.2.2.

18 ibid., section 3.2.1; see also Harris Birkeland, *The Legend of the Opening of Muhammad's Breast*, Oslo, Jacob Dybwad, 1955.

19 Jane Idleman Smith (ed.), *The Precious Pearl. A Translation from the Arabic*, Missoula, MT, Scholars Press, 1979, pp. 59, 60.

Chapter 4   Political action and theory

1 See Patricia Crone and Michael Cook, *Hagarism: the Making of the Islamic World*, Cambridge, Cambridge University Press, 1977, but cf. the many adverse reviews of the work.

2 See the (mainly unpublished) works of Yehuda D. Nevo, whose insights are

based on archeological findings in the Negev desert.

3 See G. R. Hawting, 'The significance of the slogan *la hukma illa lillah* and references to the *hudud* in the traditions about the Fitna and the murder of 'Uthman', *Bulletin of the School of Oriental and African Studies*, 41 (1978), 453–63 and his *The First Dynasty of Islam: the Umayyad Caliphate AD 661–750*, London, Croom Helm, 1986.

4 For the full text of these inscriptions see Christel Kessler, ''Abd al-Malik's inscription in the Dome of the Rock: a reconsideration', *Journal of Royal Asiatic Society*, (1970), 2–14. On the Dome in general see Oleg Grabar, 'The Umayyad Dome of the Rock in Jerusalem', *Ars Orientalis*, 3 (1959), 33–62 reprinted in his *Studies in Medieval Islamic Art*, London, Variorum, 1976, chapter 2; also his article in *Encyclopaedia of Islam, new edition*, 'al-Kuds' [=Jerusalem], part B, 'monuments'.

5 On all of these points see Grabar, 'Umayyad Dome', op. cit.; F. E. Peters, *Jerusalem and Mecca. The Typology of the Holy City in the Near East*, New York, New York University Press, 1986; Guy le Strange, *Palestine under the Moslems*, London, Palestine Exploration Fund, 1890.

6 See Peters op. cit., chapter 4.

7 See K. A. C. Creswell, *Early Muslim Architecture*, 2nd edition, Oxford, Clarendon Press, 1969, vol. 1, part 1, pp. 101–9.

8 See Howard Crosby Butler, *Early Churches in Syria, Fourth to Seventh Centuries*, Amsterdam, Adolf M. Hakkert, 1969.

9 Patricia Crone and Martin Hinds, *God's Caliph. Religious Authority in the First Centuries of Islam*, Cambridge, Cambridge University Press, 1986, but cf. the review by Norman Calder in *Journal of Semitic Studies*, 32 (1987), 375–8; also Ira M. Lapidus, 'The separation of state and religion in the development of early Islamic society', *International Journal of Middle East Studies*, 6 (1975), 363–85.

10 See Lapidus, ibid. For the role of the *'ulama'* in a somewhat later period (although still displaying precisely the same tensions as in earlier times) see Emmanuel Sivan, ''*Ulama*' and power', in his *Interpretations of Islam*, Princeton, NJ, Darwin Press, 1985, pp. 107–32.

11 Hamilton A. R. Gibb, 'Some considerations of the Sunni theory of the Caliphate', in his *Studies on the Civilization of Islam*, Boston, MA, Beacon Press, 1962, p. 148.

Chapter 5 *Theological exposition*

1 See above, chapter 4 n.3 and references.

2 See W. Madelung, 'Early Sunni doctrine concerning faith as reflected in the *Kitab al-iman* of Abu 'Ubayd al-Qasim b. Sallam (d. 224/839)', *Studia Islamica*, 32 (1970), 248–9, reprinted in his *Religious Schools and Sects in Medieval Islam*, London, Variorum, 1985. Also see J. Meric Pessagno, 'The

Murji'a, iman and Abu 'Ubayd', *Journal of the American Oriental Society*, 95 (1975), 382–94.

3 John Alden Williams (ed.), *Islam*, New York, Washington Square Press, 1963, p. 164, from the 'Epistle to 'Uthman al-Batti', slightly modified.

4 See Wilferd Madelung, 'The spread of Maturidism and the Turks', in *Actas do IV Congresso de Estudos Arabes e Islamicos, Coimbra-Lisboa 1968*, Leiden, E. J. Brill, 1971, pp. 109–68, reprinted in Madelung, op. cit., 1970.

5 See A. J. Wensinck, *The Muslim Creed, its Genesis and Historical Development*, Cambridge, Cambridge University Press, 1932, chapter 6.

6 See Williams, op. cit., pp. 162–5, although note that the full text has not been translated. Among other important texts attributed to Abu Hanifa but in fact written by his pupils, are Abu Muqatil al-Samarqandi (d. 823), *Kitab al-'alim wal-muta'allim* (see Joseph Schacht, 'An early Murci'ite treatise: the Kitab al-'alim wal-muta'allim', *Oriens*, 17 (1964), 96–117) and Abu Muti' al-Balkhi (d. 799), *al-Fiqh al-absat* (see Wensinck, op. cit., chapter 6, especially p. 123).

7 See Kenneth Cragg and Marston Speight (eds), *Islam from Within. Anthology of a Religion*, Belmont, CA, Wadsworth Publishing, 1980, p. 119, quoting from a creed ascribed to Ibn Hanbal. For a translation of another work by Ibn Hanbal, his 'Refutation of the Dualists and the Anthropomorphists', see Morris S. Seale, *Muslim Theology. A Study of Origins with reference to the Church Fathers*, 2nd edition, London, Luzac, 1980.

8 John Burton, *Abu 'Ubaid al-Qasim b. Sallam's K. al-nasikh wa-l-mansukh, edited with a commentary*, Cambridge, E. J. W. Gibb Memorial Trust, 1987, p. 46.

9 See Patricia Crone and Martin Hinds, *God's Caliph. Religious Authority in the First Centuries of Islam*, Cambridge, Cambridge University Press, 1986, especially chapter 3.

10 For some details of the debate see Michael Cook, *Early Muslim Dogma. A Source-Critical Study*, Cambridge, Cambridge University Press, 1981, chapter 12; for the text itself see the partial translation in Andrew Rippin and Jan Knappert (eds), *Textual Sources for the Study of Islam*, Manchester, Manchester University Press, 1986, section 6.1 and bibliographical references cited there.

11 Instead of 'God sends', Irving's translation of this verse and the next reads 'God lets go astray', de-emphasizing God's determination of the fate of the individual. Irving's translation reflects a modern Islamic emphasis on reading the Qur'an in light of free will.

12 See M. A. Cook, 'The origins of *kalam*', *Bulletin of the School of Oriental and African Studies*, 43 (1980), 32–43.

13 A. N. Nader (ed. and trans.), *Kitab al-Intisar. Le livre du triomphe et de la réfutation d'Ibn al-Rawandi l'hérétique par Abu al Husayn b. 'Othman al Khayyat*, Beirut, Editions les lettres Orientales, 1957, French p. 110, Arabic p. 89.

14 See Harry Austryn Wolfson, *The Philosophy of the Kalam*, Cambridge, MA, Harvard University Press, 1976, chapter 3, for a full discussion of the topic and its relationship to Jewish and Christian notions.

15 See ibid., pp. 251–5; for further discussion of the whole issue. See also Wilferd Madelung, 'The origins of the controversy concerning the creation of the Koran', in J. M. Barral (ed.), *Orientalia Hispanica sive studia F. M. Pareja octogenario dicata*, volume 1, part 1, Leiden, E. J. Brill, 1974, pp. 504–25, reprinted in Madelung, op. cit.

16 See Wolfson, op. cit., chapter 2, for a full treatment of this topic.

17 See *Encyclopaedia of Islam*, '*tashbih*' (anthropomorphism).

18 See George F. Hourani, *Islamic Rationalism. The Ethics of 'Abd al-Jabbar*, Oxford, Clarendon Press, 1971, p. 131.

19 See George F. Hourani, 'Divine justice and human reason in Mu'tazilite ethical theology', in Richard G. Hovannisian (ed.), *Ethics in Islam*, Malibu, CA, Undena Publications, 1985, pp. 73–83, especially section VII.

20 See Wilferd Madelung, 'Imamism and Mu'tazilite theology', in T. Fahd (ed.), *Le Shi'isme imamite*, Paris, Presses Universitaires de France, 1979, pp. 13–29, reprinted in Madelung, op. cit.; also see below, chapter 8.

21 Walter C. Klein (trans.), *Abu'l-Hasan 'Ali ibn Isma'il al-As'ari's al-Ibanah 'an usul ad-diyanah (The Elucidation of Islam's Foundation)*, New Haven, CT, American Oriental Society, 1940, p. 47.

22 ibid., p. 103.

23 See Richard J. McCarthy (trans.), *The Theology of al-Ash'ari*, Beirut, Imprimerie Catholique, 1953, especially chapters 1–3 of the translation of al-Ash'ari's *Kitab al-Luma'*.

24 ibid., p. 14.

25 Fathalla Kholeif (ed.), *Kitab al-tawhid. Abu Mansur Muhammad ibn Muhammad ibn Mahmud al-Maturidi al-Samarqandi*, Beirut, Dar el-Machreq Editeurs, 1970 (with an English summary of the contents); see also the studies by J. Meric Pessagno on al-Maturidi, for example, '*Irada, Ikhtiyar, Qudra, Kasb*: the view of Abu Mansur al-Maturidi', *Journal of the American Oriental Society*, 104 (1984), 177–91.

26 The creed is translated in Arthur Jeffery (ed.), *A Reader on Islam. Passages from Standard Arabic Writings illustrative of the Beliefs and Practices of Muslims*, 'S-Gravenhage, Mouton, 1962, pp. 347–52; a commentary on it by the Ash'arite al-Taftazani (d. 1388) is found in Earl Edgar Elder (trans.), *A Commentary on the Creed of Islam*, New York, Columbia University Press, 1950.

Chapter 6   Legal developments

1 See George Makdisi, 'Ash'ari and the Ash'arites in Islamic religious history', *Studia Islamica*, 17 (1962), 37–80; 18 (1963), 19–39.

2 On these terms see A. Kevin Reinhart, 'Islamic law as Islamic ethics',
   Journal of Religious Ethics, 11 (1983), 186–203. For a good over all summary
   of the development of the *usul al-fiqh*, see *Encyclopaedia of Islam*, '*fikh*', (by
   Joseph Schacht).

3 For one detailed example see Patricia Crone, *Roman, Provincial and Islamic
   Law. The Origins of the Islamic Patronate*, Cambridge, Cambridge University
   Press, 1987.

4 See Patricia Crone and Martin Hinds, *God's Caliph. Religious Authority in the
   First Centuries of Islam*, Cambridge, Cambridge University Press, 1986, pp.
   48ff.

5 See Joseph Schacht, *An Introduction to Islamic Law*, Oxford, Oxford
   University Press, 1964, pp. 17–18, 29–30.

6 See George Makdiski, 'The significance of the Sunni schools of law in Islamic
   religious history', *International Journal of Middle East Studies*, 10 (1979),
   especially p. 1.

7 For a good summary of this development see chapter 2 of Crone, op. cit.

8 For an examination of these different tendencies as displayed in specific laws,
   see Michael Cook, 'Early Islamic dietary law', *Jerusalem Studies in Arabic and
   Islam*, 7 (1986), 217–77.

9 Al-Shafi'i, *Kitab al-Umm*, Cairo, Bulaq, 1903–7, volume 7, p. 271, as
   quoted in Joseph Schacht, *The Origins of Muhammadan Jurisprudence*, Oxford,
   Oxford University Press, 1950, p. 16.

10 Al-Shafi'i, *Risala fi usul al-fiqh*, Cairo, Dar al-Ma'arif, 1940, p. 65 as quoted
   in Schacht, op. cit., 1950, p. 91.

11 On this book see N. J. Coulson, *A History of Islamic Law*, Edinburgh,
   Edinburgh University Press, 1964, pp. 43–7; there is a translation of it
   available: Imam Malik, *al-Muwatta'*, Norwich, Diwan Press, 1982.

12 See Wael B. Hallaq, 'On the authoritativeness of Sunni consensus',
   International Journal of Middle East Studies, 18 (1986), 427–54, esp. p. 448.

13 See Coulson, op. cit., p. 71.

14 See Wael B. Hallaq, 'Was the gate of ijtihad closed?' *International Journal of
   Middle East Studies*, 16 (1984), 3–41, esp. p. 10.

15 ibid., p. 11.

16 A. J. Wensinck, *The Muslim Creed, its Genesis and Historical Development*,
   Cambridge, Cambridge University Press, 1932, pp. 112–13, article 7 from
   the *Fiqh Akbar I*.

17 For further specific details on these laws and related issues, see Andrew
   Rippin and Jan Knappert (eds), *Textual Sources for the Study of Islam*,
   Manchester, Manchester University Press, 1986, section 5.1, for a text by
   al-Baghdadi (d. 1037).

18 See the discussion in Rippin and Knappert, ibid., section 5.4 on divorce.

19 See Bernard Lewis (ed. and trans.), *Islam from the Prophet Muhammad to the
   Capture of Constantinople*, volume 2: *Religion and Society*, New York, Harper &
   Row, 1974, pp. 40–2, from al-Mawardi (d. 1058).

20 As is displayed in the theological discussions over 'Uthman and 'Ali; see above chapter 5.

21 Coulson, op. cit., p. 126. Also see Norman Calder, 'Friday prayer and the juristic theory of government: Sarakhsi, Shirazi, Mawardi', *Bulletin of the School of Oriental and African Studies*, 49 (1986), 35–47.

22 For more details on these offices and several others see Reuben Levy, *The Social Structure of Islam*, Cambridge, Cambridge University Press, 1957, chapter 7.

23 A good basic overview of the legal status of the 'protected communities' is available in Majid Khadduri, *War and Peace in the Law of Islam*, Baltimore, MD, Johns Hopkins University Press, 1955, chapter 17.

Chapter 7 *Ritual practice*

1 See for example Andrew Rippin and Jan Knappert (eds), *Textual Sources for the Study of Islam*, Manchester, Manchester University Press, 1986, section 4.1 from al-Baghdadi.

2 See al-Shafi'i *Risala fi usul al-fiqh*, Cairo, Dar al-Ma'arif, 1940, p. 21, also available in English translation, Majid Khadduri (trans.) *Al-Imam Muhammad ibn Idris al-Shafi'i's Risala fi usul al-fiqh. Treatise on the Foundations of Islamic Jurisprudence*, Baltimore, Johns Hopkins, 1961 (reprint, Cambridge, Islamic Texts Society, 1987), p. 68.

3 See the (mainly unpublished) works of Yehuda D. Nevo.

4 Rippin and Knappert, op. cit., p. 90.

5 See Joseph Eliash, 'On the genesis and development of the twelver-Shi'i three-tenet shahadah', *Der Islam*, 47 (1971), 265–72.

6 See Patricia Crone and Martin Hinds, *God's Caliph. Religious Authority in the First Centuries of Islam*, Cambridge, Cambridge University Press, 1986, p. 25, n.8 and the more detailed study in John Walker, *A Catalogue of the Muhammadan Coins in the British Museum*, volumes 1 and 2, London, Trustees of the British Museum, 1941, 1956.

7 See Muslim ibn al-Hajjaj, *Sahih Muslim*, Cairo, Dar al-'Arabi, 1951, vol. I, pp. 86–8; an English translation of this work is available by Abdul Hameed Siddiqui, *Sahih Muslim*, Lahore, M. Ashraf, 1971.

8 See Edward William Lane, *An Account of the Manners and Customs of the Modern Egyptians Written in Egypt during the Years 1833–1835*, London, John Murray, 1836, pp. 69–96 for a full description (with diagrams) of the intricacies of the prayer ritual. Also see Alford T. Welch, 'Islam', in John R. Hinnells (ed.), *A Handbook of Living Religions*, Harmondsworth, Penguin, 1984, pp. 137–43.

9 See S. D. Goitein, 'Prayer in Islam', in his *Studies in Islamic History and Institutions*, Leiden, E. J. Brill, 1966, pp. 73–89 on the prayer in general, and pp. 84–5 on this specific point.

10 For an attempt at reconstructing the history of the Friday prayer see S. D. Goitein, 'The origin and development of the Muslim Friday Worship', in ibid., pp. 111–25.

11 See Rippin and Knappert, op. cit., p. 91.

12 It is quite possible for a building to be a mosque without having a minaret, however.

13 See Oleg Grabar, *The Formation of Islamic Art*, New Haven, CT, Yale University Press, 1973, pp. 121–2; the whole chapter, 'Islamic religious art: the mosque' is of central importance.

14 See Ulrich Haarmann, 'Islamic duties in history', *The Muslim World*, 68 (1978), pp. 12–13.

15 For a full treatment of the Qur'anic details on fasting see K. Wagtendonk, *Fasting in the Qur'an*, Leiden, E. J. Brill, 1968.

16 For a map of all these activities see Rippin and Knappert, op. cit., p. 93.

17 For full details on the pilgrimage including the text of the prayers see Ahmad Kamal, *The Sacred Journey, Being Pilgrimage to Makkah*, London, George Allen & Unwin, 1961. Also valuable for its pictures is Ezzedine Guellouz, *Mecca, the Muslim Pilgrimage*, London, Paddington Press, 1979.

18 See B. A. Donaldson, *The Wild Rue: a Study of Muhammadan Magic and Folklore in Iran*, London, Luzac, 1938, for information on a number of Shi'ite practices in the modern era.

19 See William Graham, 'Islam in the mirror of ritual', in Richard G. Hovannisian and Speros Vryonis Jr (eds), *Islam's Understanding of Itself*, Malibu, CA, Undena Publications, 1983, p. 69.

Chapter 8   Shi'ism

1 See John Wansbrough, *The Sectarian Milieu: Content and Composition of Islamic Salvation History*, Oxford, Oxford University Press, 1978, p. 120.

2 Quoted in Moojan Momen, *An Introduction to Shi'i Islam*, New Haven, CT, Yale University Press, 1985, p. 15.

3 See E. Kohlberg, 'Shi'i Hadith', in A. F. L. Beeston, T. M. Johnstone, R. B. Sergeant, and G. R. Smith (eds), *Arabic Literature to the End of the Umayyad Period*, Cambridge, Cambridge University Press, 1983, pp. 299–307.

4 See Abdulaziz Abdulhussein Sachedina, *Islamic Messianism. The Idea of the Mahdi in Twelver Shi'ism*, Albany, NY, State University of New York Press, 1981.

5 See E. P. Sanders, *Jesus and Judaism*, London, SCM Press, 1985, pp. 95–106.

6 See H. A. R. Gibb, 'Government and Islam under the early 'Abbasids. The political collapse of Islam,' in *L'élaboration de l'Islam*, Paris, Presses Universitaires de France, 1961, p. 118.

7   A. A. A. Fyzee, *A Shi'ite Creed. A Translation of Risalatu'l-i'tiqadat* [of Ibn Babawayh], Oxford, Oxford University Press, 1942, pp. 31–2.

8   ibid., p. 43 (translation slightly modified).

9   For the theology of al-Shaykh al-Mufid in comparison with that of the Mu'tazilites, Ibn Babawayh (Ibn Babuya) and al-Sharif al-Murtada, see Martin J. McDermott, *The Theology of al-Shaykh al-Mufid (d. 413/1022)*, Beirut, Dar el-Machreq, 1978. Also see Wilferd Madelung, 'Imamism and Mu'tazilite theology', in T. Fahd (ed.), *Le Shi'isme imamite*, Paris, Presses Universitaires de France, 1979, pp. 13–29, reprinted in his *Religious Schools and Sects in Medieval Islam*, London, Variorum, 1985.

10 See Momen, op. cit., p. 189.

11 See Norman Calder, 'Judicial authority in Imami Shi'i jurisprudence', *British Society for Middle Eastern Studies Bulletin*, 6 (1979), 104–8. Also see Wilferd Madelung, 'Authority in Twelver Shiism in the absence of the Imam', in *La notion d'authorité au moyen age: Islam, Byzance, Occident. Colloques internationaux de la Napoule 1978*, Paris, Presses Universitaires de France, 1982, pp. 163–73, reprinted in Madelung, op. cit.

12 For details more on juridical development in Shi'ism see Norman Calder, 'Zakat in Imami Shi'i jurisprudence, from the tenth to the sixteenth century A.D.', *Bulletin of the School of Oriental and African Studies*, 44 (1981), 468–80, and his 'Khums in Imami Shi'i jurisprudence, from the tenth to the sixteenth century A.D.', *Bulletin of the School of Oriental and African Studies*, 45 (1982), 39–47.

13 See Fyzee, op. cit., p. 61.

14 See Mahmoud Ayoub, *Redemptive Suffering in Islam. A Study of the devotional Aspects of 'Ashura' in Twelver Shi'ism*, The Hague, Mouton, 1978.

Chapter 9   Sufism

1   See Andrew Rippin and Jan Knappert (eds), *Textual Sources for the Study of Islam*, Manchester, Manchester University Press, 1986, section 7.2.2. for an Isma'ili, mystically-flavoured interpretation of this passage.

2   See ibid., section 8.1, for extracts from this text.

3   See Ignaz Goldziher, *Muslim Studies*, London, George Allen & Unwin, 1971, vol. 2, pp. 356–60.

4   See Norman Calder, '*Hinth, birr, tabarrur, tahannuth*: an inquiry into the Arabic vocabulary of vows', *Bulletin of the School of Oriental and African Studies*, 51 (1988), 214–39.

5   See Margaret Smith, *An Early Mystic of Baghdad*, London, Sheldon Press, 1935; also Ignaz Goldziher, *Introduction to Islamic Theology and Law*, Princeton, NJ, Princeton University Press, 1981, p. 130, citing a study of D. S. Margoliouth.

6   For a treatment of a developed formulation of the *dhikr*, see Hamid Algar,

'Silent and vocal *dhikr* in the Naqshbandi order', in Albert Dietrich (ed.), *Akten der VII. Kongresses für Arabistik und Islamwissenschaft*, Göttingen, Vandenhoeck & Ruprecht, 1976, pp. 39–46.

7   Ali Hassan Abdel-Kader, *The Life, Personality and Writings of al-Junayd*, London, Luzac, 1976, p. 89, quoting from al-Junayd, *al-Risala*.

8   For further information on this type of Sufism see Carl W. Ernst, *Words of Ecstasy in Sufism*, Albany, NY, State University of New York Press, 1985.

9   Margaret Smith (ed. and trans.), *Readings from the Mystics of Islam*, London, Luzac, 1950, p. 43.

10   See Seyyed Hossein Nasr, 'The spiritual states in Sufism', in his *Sufi Essays*, New York, Schocken Books, 1977, pp. 68–83 and A. J Arberry, *Sufism, an Account of the Mystics of Islam*, London, George Allen & Unwin, 1950, chapter 7.

11   Al-Ghazzali, *Bidayat al-hidayah*, translated in W. Montgomery Watt, *The Faith and Practice of al-Ghazali*, Lahore, Sh. Muhammad Ashraf, 1963, p. 90.

12   See J. Spencer Trimingham, *The Sufi Orders in Islam*, Oxford, Oxford University Press, 1971, p. 14 and passim for further information.

13   This anecdote in taken from Mtungaji Mwinyi H. Mzale, *Sayyid Abdul Kadir na karama zake*, Zanzibar, 1968, unpublished translation by J. Knappert. For other examples of these ancecdotes see Rippin and Knappert, op. cit., section 8.3.

14   See Rippin and Knappert, op. cit., section 8.4.

15   See Canon Sell, *The Religious Orders of Islam*, Madras and London, SPCK, 1908, p. 40. For more information on general Sufi practices, see Jean-Louis Michon, 'The spiritual practices of Sufism', in Seyyed Hossein Nasr (ed.), *Islamic Spirituality. Foundations*, New York, Crossroads, 1987, pp. 265–93.

16   See the many works of Henry Corbin, for example, his *Creative Imagination in the Sufism of Ibn 'Arabi*, Princeton, NJ, Princeton University Press, 1969.

Chapter 10   Conclusion

1   Edgar V. McKnight, *Post-Modern Use of the Bible. The Emergence of Reader-Oriented Criticism*, Nashville, TN, Abingdon Press, 1988, p. 108.

Further reading

The notes to each chapter should be consulted for additional references. The following is only a general reading list, composed of some of the more significant and informative works for the study of Islam.

Arberry, A.J., *Sufism. An Account of the Mystics of Islam*, London, George Allen & Unwin, 1950.

Cook, Michael, *Muhammad*, Oxford, Oxford University Press, 1983.

——, *Early Muslim Dogma. A Source-Critical Study*, Cambridge, Cambridge University Press, 1981.

Crone, Patricia, *Meccan Trade and the Rise of Islam*, Princeton, NJ, Princeton University Press, 1987.

Crone, Patricia, and Cook, Michael, *Hagarism. The Making of the Islamic World*, Cambridge, Cambridge University Press, 1977.

Crone, Patricia, and Hinds, Martin, *God's Caliph. Religious Authority in the First Centuries of Islam*, Cambridge, Cambridge University Press, 1986.

von Denffer, Ahmad, *'Ulum al-Qur'an. An Introduction to the Sciences of the Qur'an*, Leicester, The Islamic Foundation, 1983.

Ede, David, Librande, Leonard, Little, Donald P., Rippin, Andrew, Timms, Richard, and Weryho, Jan, *Guide to Islam*, Boston, G. K. Hall, 1983. [A good bibliographical tool.]

van Ess, Josef, 'The beginnings of Islamic theology', in Murdoch, J. E., and Sylla, E. D. (eds), *The Cultural Context of Medieval Learning*, Dordrecht, D. Reidel Publishing, 1975, pp. 87–111.

——, 'Early development of *Kalam*', in Juynboll, G. H. A. (ed.), *Studies on the First Century of Islamic Society*, Carbondale, IL, Southern Illinois University

Press, 1982, pp. 109–23. [Most of van Ess' works, all of which are essential to the study of Islamic theology, are written in German; these two articles, however, do provide a good introduction to his perspective.]

Goldziher, Ignaz, *Introduction to Islamic Theology and Law*, Princeton, NJ, Princeton University Press, 1981.

——, *Muslim Studies*, 2 vols, London, George Allen & Unwin, 1966–71.

——, *The Zahiris, their Doctrine and their History*, Leiden, E. J. Brill, 1971.

Grabar, Oleg, *The Formation of Islamic Art*, New Haven, CT, Yale University Press, 1973.

Groom, Nigel, *Frankincense and Myrrh. A Study of the Arabian Incense Trade*, London, Longman, 1981.

von Grunebaum, G. E., *Classical Islam. A History 600 AD – 1258 AD*, Chicago, IL, Aldine Publishing, 1970.

——, *Muhammadan Festivals*, New York, Henry Schuman, 1951.

Hawting, G. R., *The First Dynasty of Islam. The Umayyad Caliphate AD 661 – 750*, London, Croom Helm, 1986.

Kohlberg, E., 'From Imamiya to Ithna-'ashariyya', *Bulletin of the School of Oriental and African Studies*, 39 (1976), 521–34.

Kuban, Dogan, *Muslim Religious Architecture*, 2 parts, Leiden, E. J. Brill, 1974–85.

Lewis, Bernard, *The Arabs in History*, 4th edition, London, Hutchinson, 1966.

Madelung, Wilferd, *Religious Schools and Sects in Medieval Islam*, London, Variorum, 1985.

Momen, Moojan, *An Introduction to Shi'i Islam*, New Haven, CT, Yale University Press, 1985. [An excellent work, unexcelled in its field, suitable for all readers.]

Nasr, Seyyed Hossein (ed.), *Islamic Spirituality. Foundations*, New York, Crossroads, 1987. [Especially useful for the chapters on Sufism.]

Parrinder, Geoffrey, *Jesus in the Qur'an*, London, Faber & Faber, 1965.

Rahman, Fazlur, *Islam*, 2nd edition, Chicago, IL, The University of Chicago Press, 1979.

——, *Major Themes of the Qur'an*, Chicago, IL, Bibliotheca Islamica, 1980. [Both of these works by Rahman provide a good overview of the subject from a critical modernist Muslim standpoint.]

Schacht, Joseph, *The Origins of Muhammadan Jurisprudence*, Oxford, Clarendon Press, 1950. [Technical, but essential to all advanced studies.]

——, *An Introduction to Islamic Law*, Oxford, Clarendon Press, 1964.

Schacht, Joseph, and Bosworth, C. E. (eds), *The Legacy of Islam*, 2nd edition, Oxford, Oxford University Press, 1979.

Schimmel, Annemarie, *And Muhammad is His Messenger. The Veneration of the Prophet in Islamic Piety*, Chapel Hill, NC, The University of North Carolina Press, 1985.

——, *Mystical Dimensions of Islam*, Chapel Hill, NC, The University of North Carolina Press, 1975.

Shahid, Irfan, 'Pre-Islamic Arabia', in Holt, P. M., Lambton, A. K. S., and Lewis, B. (eds), *The Cambridge History of Islam*, vol. 1, Cambridge, Cambridge University Press, 1970, pp. 3–29.

Smith, Margaret, *Rabi'a the Mystic and her Fellow-Saints in Islam*, Cambridge, Cambridge University Press, 1928, reprinted 1984.

Watt, W. M., *The Formative Period of Islamic Thought*, Edinburgh, Edinburgh University Press, 1973.

Stanton, H. U. W., *The Teaching of the Qur'an, with an Account of its Growth and a Subject Index*, London, SPCK, 1919, reprinted 1969.

Swartz, Merlin (ed.), *Studies on Islam*, New York and Oxford, Oxford University Press, 1981.

Trimingham, J. S., *The Sufi Orders in Islam*, Oxford, Oxford University Press, 1971.

Wansbrough, John, *Quranic Studies. Sources and Methods of Scriptural Interpretation*, Oxford, Oxford University Press, 1977. [Essential for all advanced students.]

——, *The Sectarian Milieu. Content and Composition of Islamic Salvation History*, Oxford, Oxford University Press, 1978.

Wensinck, A. J., *The Muslim Creed. Its Genesis and Historical Development*, Cambridge, Cambridge University Press, 1932.

Index

151

Index

Index of Qur'an citations